The Archaeology of Guyana

Mark G. Plew

BAR International Series 1400
2005

Published in 2016 by
BAR Publishing, Oxford

BAR International Series 1400

The Archaeology of Guyana

ISBN 978 1 84171 839 2

© M G Plew and the Publisher 2005

The author's moral rights under the 1988 UK Copyright,
Designs and Patents Act are hereby expressly asserted.

All rights reserved. No part of this work may be copied, reproduced, stored,
sold, distributed, scanned, saved in any form of digital format or transmitted
in any form digitally, without the written permission of the Publisher.

BAR Publishing is the trading name of British Archaeological Reports (Oxford) Ltd.
British Archaeological Reports was first incorporated in 1974 to publish the BAR
Series, International and British. In 1992 Hadrian Books Ltd became part of the BAR
group. This volume was originally published by Archaeopress in conjunction with
British Archaeological Reports (Oxford) Ltd / Hadrian Books Ltd, the Series principal
publisher, in 2005. This present volume is published by BAR Publishing, 2016.

Printed in England

BAR titles are available from:

        BAR Publishing
        122 Banbury Rd, Oxford, OX2 7BP, UK
EMAIL   info@barpublishing.com
PHONE +44 (0)1865 310431
FAX   +44 (0)1865 316916
        www.barpublishing.com

Table of Contents

Acknowledgments		v
Introduction		vii
I.	A History and Overview of Archaeological Research in Guyana	1
II.	The Natural Setting	2
III.	The Ethnographic Context	4
IV.	Guyana Chronologies	6
V.	Pleistocene-Holocene Environmental Change	9
VI.	The Early Peopling of Guyana: The Evidence for Paleo-Indian Hunters and Early Archaic Foragers in the Rupununi Savannahs	11
	Summary	12
VII.	The Archaeology of Northwestern Guyana: Archaic Shellfishers and Early Horticulturalists of the Littoral	13
	The Archaeology of Barabina Shell Mound	17
	Horticultural Origins in Northwestern Guyana: A Re-Characterization of the Mabaruma Phase	19
	Excavations at Hosororo Creek	20
	Summary	22
VIII.	The Archaeology of the Northeast	23
	The Abary Phase	23
	Earthen Mounds: Archaeological Evidence of Habitation Mounds and Raised Fields	23
	Summary	25
IX.	The Archaeology of Southeastern Guyana: The Taruma Phase	27
	Rock Art of the Kassikaityu: Archaeological Evidence of Fisheries Management?	27
	The Wai-Wai Archaeological Phase	29
	Summary	30
X.	The Archaeology of the Rupununi Savannah	33
	The Paleo-Indian Period	33
	The Archaic Period	33
	The Rock Art of Aishalton	33
	The Horticultural Period	35
	The Shiriri Mountain Survey	36
	Stone Alignments in the Rupununi	36
	The Archaeology of Shiriri Mountain Cemetery	39
	Recent Archaeological Surveys in the Vicinity of the Kanuku Mountains	41
	Archaeological Sites Near Shulinab and Mariwau: Further Evidence of Rupununi Funerary Practices.	42
	The Archaeology of Toka and Yupukari	45
	Summary	45

XI. The Central Guyana Rainforest: Archaeology in Iwokrama	47
The Paleo-Indian Period	47
The Archaic Period	47
Groundstone Features	51
Lithic Chipping/Manufacturing Station	51
Archaic Sites in the Iwokrama Mountains	52
Horticultural Period	52
Essequibo River	53
The Ceramic Inventory	53
Siparuni River	56
Summary	58
XII. Guyana Prehistory in Review	61
References Cited	64

List of Tables

Table 1.	Radiocarbon Dates for Guyana Archaeological Sites	7
Table 2.	Barabina Shell Mound. Unit 4: Fish and Shellfish Remains/Level (g)	20
Table 3.	Barabina Shell Mound, Burial Frequencies; Upper Limb Flexture/Level; Orientation	20
Table 4.	Classification of Excavation Levels According to Phase in Cut 3 at Hososoro Creek	21
Table 5.	Classification of Motifs of the Aishalton Complex	37
Table 6.	Groundstone Features Near Imprenza	42
Table 7.	Ceramic Vessels from Site IX-2-91	44
Table 8.	Distribution of Rupununi Phase Sites by Type.	46
Table. 9.	Iwokrama Petroglyph Sites	50
Table 10.	Distribution of Basin Depressions and Sharpening Grooves by Drainage and Site	51
Table 11.	Big 'S' Falls (VIII-2.39): Relationships of Length to Depth in 118 Sharpening Grooves	52
Table 12.	Radiocarbon Dates from Kurupukari and Makari Falls	55
Table 13.	VIII-2.23 Kurupukari Falls. Sherd Frequencies/Level	55
Table 14.	General Chronology of Iwokrama Sites	59

List of Figures

Figure 1.	Map of Guyana Showing Mountain Ranges and Major Rivers	3
Figure 2.	Map Showing Locations of Tribal Groups in Guyana	4
Figure 3.	Major Archaeological Phases of Guyana	6
Figure 4.	Radiocarbon Dated Sites	8
Figure 5.	Seba Creek Profile	9
Figure 6.	Amazonian *refugia*	10
Figure 7.	Paleo-Indian Type Points from Guyana	11
Figure 8.	Paleo-Indian Points from Guyana	12
Figure 9.	Alaka and Mabaruma Phase Sites	14
Figure 10.	Scrapers from the Alaka Phase	15
Figure 11.	Alaka Phase Slate Picks	16
Figure 12.	Aruka Ceramic Forms	17
Figure 13.	Mabaruma Phase Kaituma Incised and Punctate	18
Figure 14.	Mabaruma Phase Akawabi Incised and Modeled	18
Figure 15.	Map Showing Location of Barabina and Other Mounds of the Northwest	19
Figure 16.	Early Formative Vessel Forms from Hosororo Creek	21
Figure 17.	Abary Phase Sites	24
Figure 18.	Vessel Forms and Barancoid-Like Adornos from Recht-door-Zee	25
Figure 19.	Raised Horticultural Plots on the Berbice-Canje Watershed.	26
Figure 20.	Taruma Phase Sites	28
Figure 21.	Kalunye Plain Vessel and Rim Forms	29
Figure 22.	Decorated Pottery of the Taruma Phase	31
Figure 23.	Fish Trap Petroglyphs on the Kassikaityu	32
Figure 24.	Wai-Wai Phase Ceramics	32
Figure 25.	Selected Archaeological Sites of the Rupununi	34
Figure 26.	Granite Boulders near Aishalton	35
Figure 27.	Rock Art Designs on Boulders Near Makatau Cave	35
Figure 28.	Kanuku and Rupununi Phase Vessel Forms	38
Figure 29.	Stone Alignment at Lukobar Mountain	39
Figure 30.	Shiriri Mountain Cemetery with Ceramic Vessels in Foreground	40
Figure 31.	Sealed Vessel, Shiriri Mountain Cemetery	40
Figure 32.	Painted Vessel from Shiriri Mountain	41
Figure 33.	Groundstone Features Near Imprenza	43
Figure 34.	Cairn Burial Near Moco-Moco...	43
Figure 35.	Burial Vessels at Rockshelter Near Shulinab Village	43
Figure 36.	Burial Vessels from Site Near Mariwau	44
Figure 37.	Artifacts from Toka Village...	45
Figure 38.	General Location of the Iwokrama Reserve	48
Figure 39.	Map Showing the Location of Archaeological Sites within Iwokrama	49
Figure 40.	Tertiary Stream, East Face, Iwokrama Mountains	51
Figure 41.	Kurukupari Falls. Rock Art Covered Boulders in Foreground	54
Figure 42.	General Vessel Forms from Kurupukari	56
Figure 43.	Kurupukari Incised and Modeled	57

Acknowledgments

I am indebted to a number of individuals and agencies whose assistance has been invaluable during the preparation of this manuscript. First, the Department of Anthropology, Boise State University, provided support throughout the writing of the book and provided funds to assist with the preparation of illustrations. My Guyanese colleagues have provided valuable commentary on the ideas developed here. In particular, Gerard Pereira, Walter Roth Museum of Anthropology, has helped me think more critically about the intricacies of Guyana prehistory. Minister Gail Teixeira, the Ministry of Culture, Youth and Sport, Republic of Guyana, has been deeply committed to preserving the cultural heritage of Guyana. Her support for our efforts over a number of years is very much appreciated. Likewise, Jennifer Wishart, Amerindian Research Unit, University of Guyana, has provided much assistance over the past several years. I am indebted in particular to Dr. Betty Meggers for her review of an earlier draft of the book. Dr. Meggers' critical evaluation has greatly improved the quality and substance of the work. Barbara Valdez edited several versions of the manuscript. Her efforts have brought greater clarity to the text. Additional edits were provided by Faith Brigham. Shelby Day provided a number of illustrations and Chris Willson assisted in preparing the tables. Finally, and most importantly, I wish to acknowledge an intellectual debt to the late Dr. Denis Williams whose life long commitment to Guyana archaeology has been an inspiration.

M.P.

Introduction

Though Amazonian archaeology has seen considerable development in the past 25 years, knowledge of vast portions of the area remains relatively limited (Whitehead 1996). This is very much the case with the Guianas generally and with Guyana in particular. Though archaeological investigations date from the late 19th century, much of what is known of Guyana prehistory is known from work begun in the late 1940's under the direction of Cornelius Osgood (1946) and subsequently undertaken in the early 1950's by Clifford Evans and Betty Meggers (1960). Beginning in the late 1970's, Guyanese archaeologist Denis Williams conducted surveys and excavations in various parts of the country. More recently Mark Plew and Gerard Pereria, in collaboration with several Guyanese scholars, have conducted investigations in various areas of the Rupununi Savannahs and in the Iwokrama rainforest. While the results of investigations of Evans and Meggers (1960) are well-known, the more recent work is relatively unknown beyond Guyana. This book attempts to provide a broadly based summary of the archaeology that integrates the frameworks provided by Osgood (1946), Evans and Meggers (1960) and Williams (1985b, 1995, n.d.) within a standard archaeological format and considers more recent archaeological investigations.

As with other regional summaries, this work builds upon earlier syntheses, notable among them that by Evans and Meggers (1960), which remains in many ways the major outline of Guyana prehistory. Following the work by Evans and Meggers (1960), no significant archaeological research was conducted in Guyana until the 1970's when Denis Williams initiated a program of field investigations. This led to the publication of two short general summaries. The first of these, *Ancient Guyana* (1985), summarizes the work of Evans and Meggers while integrating the findings of his investigations conducted between 1978 and 1985; it was followed by the popular publication *Pages in Guyanese Prehistory* (1995). In addition, Williams' (2004) posthumously published *Prehistoric Guiana* provides a comprehensive and highly descriptive overview of the archaeology of the Guianas. It includes numerous interpretations of rock art and of Amazonian archaeology. His work is highlighted in *A Look at the Archaeology of Guyana: 50 Years After.* Osgood prepared by the Amerindian Research Unit, University of Guyana and the Guyana National Trust. This brief paper provides a compendium of sites and maps relating to the archaeology of the country (2003). Finally, Plew and Forte (1998) published *A Bibliography of Guyana Anthropology* that lists extensive archaeological references, including many generally unknown.

This book is written for professional archaeologists, students of South American archaeology, heritage managers, museum staffs, and the general public. The book intends to provide sufficient breadth and detail that it stands as a scholarly work, while presenting data in a manner which allows for a wide use of the materials. Thus the book summarizes well-known sites and those less known but important to understanding the regional prehistory. This is made difficult by the fact that the history of archaeological investigations is uneven since only limited investigations have been conducted over the past century and these for a variety of reasons. In many instances the work has been reported only sporadically and incompletely. As a result, only a few sites are well-known and fewer completely reported. In addition, the long-standing historical orientation of Guyana archaeology has tended to focus on a few specific sites as primary points of interpretation.

The primary objective of this book is to craft an overview and synthesis of the archaeology of Guyana and in so doing document the diversity of human adaptations over several thousands of years. While some may disagree with areal and topical emphases or the interpretation of specific contexts or problems, hopefully all will find utility in the broad summaries provided here.

The book attempts to bring some balance between descriptive analysis of specific sites and the overall sub-regional archaeology of the area. It relies upon data derived from excavated sites and survey results and makes wide use of significant published and unpublished data since much significant work remains a part of Guyana's "gray" literature. A chronology that includes Paleo-Indian, Archaic, and Horticultural periods is used as an organizing framework. This framework, though useful in discussing changes in material cultures in time and space, does not provide adequate means by which to assess the dynamics of prehistoric cultural adaptations. However, the strongly historical tradition of Guyana archaeology, coupled with the incomparability of many data sets, renders a cultural-historical framework the most realistic at present. The archaeology of each major area within Guyana is considered. Each temporal period is introduced and discussed with respect to specific investigations. Each major site is discussed as to age, context, depositional/post-depositional histories, assemblage variation, ecofactual data including botanical and faunal remains, and raw materials sources. In some instances, discussion is relatively detailed if little is known or published on a particular area. Such is the case with the Iwokrama rainforest, where archaeological investigations have not been fully published. Though this overview is largely developmental in scope, it does where appropriate discuss problems and issues in Guyanese prehistory. Among these are the early peopling of Guyana, the origins of pottery-making shellfisher cultures, and the beginnings of horticulture in the Northwest. Discussions are developed in instances where a particular site or discovery has been the subject of

INTRODUCTION

a particular site or discovery has been the subject of debate. Material cultures, archaeological patterns, and features such as rock art and rock alignments that are common to the region as a whole or specific to a particular region are exemplified. Sub-regions include the Northwest, Northeast, Southeast, Iwokrama Rain Forest, and the South Rupununi Savannahs.

The book consists of ten chapters. Chapter One provides an historical overview of the history of archaeological research in Guyana during the late 19th century and late 20th century, including institutional developments and theoretical and methodological orientations. Chapter Two provides an overview of the geological history, climate and geography while Chapter Three briefly outlines the ethnographic context. Chapter Four discusses the general chronological context of Guyana prehistory, and Chapter Five summarizes the Late Pleistocene/Early Holocene paleo-environmental context as it relates to early human settlement of the region. Chapter Six summarizes the evidence for Paleo-Indian occupations, while Chapter Seven reviews the prehistory of Northwestern Guyana with specific reference to the Archaic shellfisher and later Horticultural patterns of the littoral. Chapter Eight summarizes the archaeology of the Abary and Hertenrits Phases of Northeastern Guyana, and Chapter Nine provides an overview of the Taruma Phase of Southeastern Guyana. Chapter Ten summarizes the Paleo-Indian, Archaic, and Horticultural occupations of the Rupununi savannahs. Chapter Eleven provides summary and synthesis of the Iwokrama rainforest in central Guyana, and Chapter Twelve reviews major developments in Guyana archaeology and future research needs.

I. A History and Overview of Archaeological Research in Guyana

The history of archaeological research in Guyana provides a chronological/developmental framework of the area's prehistory and documents the beginning of scientific archaeology in Guyana. Though notable scholars, including Schomburgk (1841), Farabee (1918, 1924), and Roth (1924) refer to archaeological sites, particularly petroglyphs, the pioneers in Guyanese archaeology are Brett (1868) and Im Thurn (1884). Their excavations of the Waramuri mounds and observations about the distribution and relatedness of material cultures are among the earliest formal investigations. These early accounts brought several excavators to the northeast and northwest regions, where a number of coastal sites were investigated early in the 20th century. Many of these early accounts, including that by Toro (1905), report elaborate sites characterized by quartz utensils, pottery adornos, and burial urns but provide little descriptive context. Generally characterized by a lack of systematic investigation, the late 19th and early 20th century in Guyanese archaeology must be considered a period of considerable speculation.

One of the first archaeologists to bring descriptive synthesis to the prehistory of Guyana was Verrill (1918), who discussed the material and geographic variability of the coastal mounds. Defining variations in "hilltop" and "shell heap" sites, he provided the first good descriptions of such notable sites as Akawabi, Kumaka, Koriabo, and Barabina, where he estimated shell mass at some 5 billion shells. He concluded that two distinct patterns existed: a lowland coastal pattern like that in the Pomeroon region and a second pattern situated on hilltops distant from the coast. While his speculations regarding the origins, migrations, and habits of these early coastal peoples remain untenable, his descriptions of site contexts and material remains are important. Equally important are his (1918) investigations of sites in the Demerara area, particularly along the Abary River.

The beginnings of what may be termed the descriptive-historic period in Guyanese archaeology are marked by Cornelius Osgood's 1944 explorations in the Northwest and Demerara regions. Asserting an Arawak affiliation for the peoples of the Northwest District, he noted similarities between Demerara style potteries and the Los Barrancos style to the west and argued that people lived on hilltop sites rather than using them exclusively for ceremonial functions, as had been suggested by Verrill. Osgood's (1946) subsequent investigations are the first to adequately document such excavations and to suggest the need for a more rigorous and systematic approach.

Following Osgood, in 1960 Evans and Meggers undertook the most regionally comprehensive investigations to that date. During several months in the field in 1952, they visited the Rupununi Savannah, the Mabaruma area in the northwest, the Abary River area in the Northeast, and the Taruma country along the upper Essequibo River in southeastern Guyana. Their investigations resulted in the development of several phase chronologies, including the definition of the Rupununi and Taruma phases, among others, and the description of many ceramic types. Following these investigations, little archaeological research was conducted until the 1970's, when Williams initiated a series of studies in both the north and south of the country.

The range of Williams' work is broad, but his more important contributions include a discussion of petroglyphs associated with fisheries management (1985a) and of the origins of horticulture in the Northwest (Williams 1992), particularly as related to technological change. This work is largely history, though it contains ecological considerations in analyses that provide insights regarding the varied use of resources within the tropical environment. This is particularly true in his assessments of the prehistory of the shell middens in northwest Guyana.

In recent years Plew and Pereira (2000, 2002) have conducted extensive surveys and test excavations at several locations throughout the southern savannahs. These surveys have identified a wider range of archaeological site types than those described earlier by Evans and Meggers. In addition, Plew's (2002, 2003) surveys and test excavations in the Iwokrama rainforest reserve suggest a broader use than previously recorded. In spite of a history of archaeology that spans more than a century, the prehistory of the region remains very much in a pioneering stage.

II. The Natural Setting

Guyana is characterized by considerable variation in landforms, climate, floral, and faunal distributions. The modern and paleo-environmental contexts provide by analogy useful insights regarding land use by Amerindians and establish a baseline from which the impact of long-term environmental and cultural changes may be assessed.

Guyana consists of a landmass of almost 197,000 square kilometers, a geographic area comparable to that of Idaho. Situated on the northeastern coast of South America, it possesses an Atlantic coastline of some 430 kilometers and is bounded by Venezuela on the west, Suriname on the east, and Brazil on the west and south. Geologically, it consists of a coastal plain, a white sand belt, and interior highlands. The coastal plain consists of alluvial sediments washed into the ocean from the Amazon River and deposited on the Guyanese coastline. These contain extensive clays overlain by white sand and clay resulting from erosion of bedrocks carried to the coast by interior rivers. The plain itself extends some 5-6 kilometers inland from the Atlantic along the entire coastline. Though constituting less than five percent of the total landmass, the coastal plain presently contains more than 90 percent of the non-Amerindian population. Near the Atlantic it contains extensive mudflats and mangrove swamps, many parts of which are inundated during high tide.

South of the coastal plain, white sand formations cover an area between 150 and 250 miles wide. Created from interior erosion of bedrocks, the white sands are characterized by low-lying sand hills, rocky outcrops, and dense forest. Erosion is rapid and has been increased by bauxite, gold, and diamond mining common in the region. Beyond the white sands are the interior highlands, Guyana's largest geological area, characterized by high plateaus, mountains, and savannahs. While much of the southern portion of the interior highlands includes the expansive grasslands (ca. 15,000 square kilometers) of the Rupununi Savannah, the western portion is dominated by the Pakaraima Mountains. Formed by the uplift of some of the oldest sedimentary formations on the continent, the Pakaraimas include Mount Roraima on the Venezuelan border, at 2,762 m Guyana's highest peak. South of the Pakaraimas, the Kaiteur Plateau rises to nearly 600 m and further south, the Kanuku Mountains reach elevations of 1,000 m. The Kanuku, like the Pakaraimas, have heavy forest cover broken by areas of exposed granite. Many parts of the interior, including the savannahs, are characterized by highly lateritic soils.

The coastal plain, the white sands belt and interior highlands are drained by several generally north-south flowing rivers. The exception is eastern Guyana, where rivers flow in an easterly direction into the Essequibo. These include the Cuyuni and the Mazaruni Rivers. These rivers drain the Kaiteur Plateau, while the Essequibo, the country's largest river, drains the majority of the interior basin. In the Northwest, the Barima, Waini, and Pomeroon Rivers parallel the coastal plain before draining into the Atlantica. In the northeast, a number of small rivers, including the Abary and Koriabo, flow north into the Atlantica. Draining into the Essequibo in the south are the Rupununi, Kuyuwini, and Kassikaityu Rivers. The western Brazilian and Venezuelan borders include the Takatu and Ireng Rivers, which flow south. The major river of the eastern region is the Berbice upon which rapids and waterfalls limit upstream transport. Among the most noted hydrological features of the country is the Kaiteur Falls on the Potaro River, which descends 226 m. Water types include whitewater, black water, and clear water (see Sinoli 1984). Whitewater is yellowish-colored because of a heavy sediment load, while clear water appears green to olive-green and carries low levels of suspended sediments and organics. Clear waters are transparent to depths of more than 4 m. Black waters, which are olive to reddish-brown from humic and fluvic acids carried in solution, are transparent to depths of about 3 m. Whitewater is common in lower elevations, on the coastal plains and in major rivers including the Essequibo, Demerara and the Courtyne. Black waters are typical in forested regions, whereas clear waters occur in the interior highlands.

Climatically, Guyana lies south of the Caribbean hurricane belt and is influenced greatly by the northeast trade winds. The country is characterized by a tropical climate, high temperatures, and rainfall which varies little seasonally. The most significant variation is between dry and wet seasons, though levels of rainfall also vary between the coast and interior highlands. Generally, the heaviest rains fall in the Northwest of Guyana and rainfall is significantly less in the interior and southeast. Yet, rainfall levels in the Iwokrama Forest of central Guyana range between a high of more than 420 inches in May (rainy season, May to July) and 55 in November. Rainfall levels in the Rupununi Savannah are typically somewhat lower. Temperatures there remain relatively constant though varying slightly between wet and dry seasons. During the hottest months, they vary between 32° C and 24° C, with slightly lower ranges during the cooler months of the year (February). Humidity averages approximately 70% year round.

The distribution of flora and fauna reflects the variability of the landscapes of Guyana. Lowland areas near the coast are typically characterized by mangrove swamps and low lying vegetation. Beyond the coast, mixed and Mora forests create extensive canopy that is characteristic of some two-thirds of the country. The vegetation of the interior highlands varies depending upon location, elevation, and drainage but typically is mixed-Mora forest. The Ité palm common throughout the area serves as a source of food and materials. The mountain ranges of the savannah are characteristically mixed forest, while the savannahs consist of native grasses and shrubs and are dotted with sandpaper trees. Several varieties of manioc, banana, and plaintain are grown throughout the area. Many types of fruits, nuts, and vegetables are common in the forested regions as well as in the savannahs of the south. The savannahs, however, produce guave and cashews, which do not grow well in the wetter regions.

Native fauna includes peccaries, capaybara, tapir, laba, agouti, armadillo, opossum, giant anteater, sloth, giant river otter, and a wide range of small rodents. Jaguars and several varieties of primates inhabit the forested regions. Avifauna, which is extremely diverse, particularly in the Kanuku Mountains of the Rupununi, includes Harpy Eagles. In addition, Guyana is noted for its diverse aquatic species which include pirhana, pacu, arawana, lukunani, and arapaima, the world's largest freshwater fish. Manatees, freshwater dolphins, river turtles, and the giant black cayman are well established.

Figure 1. Map of Guyana Showing Mountain Ranges and Major Rivers

III. The Ethnographic Context

The Amerindian population of Guyana consists of ten groups which include three coastal and seven interior tribes. They are distinguished by language and culture but are socio-politically similar, each exhibiting highly individualistic social structure (see Rivière 1984 for discussion). Ethnographic documentation began in the late 19th century with Im Thurn's *Among the Indians of Guiana* (1983). In the early 20th century, Walter Roth conducted extensive ethnographic studies that resulted in the publication of a number of important surveys (1915,

Figure 2. Map Showing Locations of Tribal Groups in Guyana

1924, 1929). During the same interval, in 1918 and 1924, Farabee conducted fieldwork in southern Guyana. In the 1930's Gillen (1936) conducted extensive research among the Barama River Caribs. Following a brief hiatus during which minor studies were conducted among the Wapishana (see Meyers 1944, 1946), systematic investigations were again begun in the 1950's with Butt's 1954 study of the Akawaio. Butt (Butt-Colson) continued to publish extensively on various aspects of Akawaio culture through the 1980's. In the 1950's and early 1960's, Fock (1963) and Yde (1965) published accounts of the lifeways and material culture of the Wai-Wai. This work was expanded upon by Mentor (1984, 1988, 1995). More recently, Forte has published extensively on Makushi and Wapishana and on issues related to contemporary Amerindians (1989, 1996a, 1996b). Menezes (1979) has published widely on the history of Amerindians.

The coastal groups consist of Carib, Arawak, and Warau tribes whose names are derived from the three language families of Guyana. The remnant Carib population is largely coastal, while Arawak are found to the west in the vicinity of the Pomeroon River, and the Warau are located in eastern Guyana near the Couretyne River. The interior tribes include the Akawaio, Arekuna, Barama River Caribs, and the Patamona, who inhabit the northwestern portion of Guyana. The Makushi, Wapishana, and Wai-Wai tribes are inhabitants of the southern savannahs. The Wai-Wai tribe is found in southern Guyana in what was formerly Taruma territory and in Brazil.

The settlement-subsistence regimes of the Amerindian populations vary somewhat by environmental context. The most obvious distinctions are between forest populations and those of the southern savannahs though groups were generally autonomous, as Rivière (1984) has observed. The northern forested regions are inhabited by populations living in small villages along major river courses. Villages consist of several households that cultivate manioc and a range of other plants, hunt local game--which is often scarce--and make use of the extensive fishery. Garden plots and more extensive fields tend to be located within relatively short distances of dwellings. Variation in subsistence correlates with dry/wet seasons, which make resources either plentiful or relatively scarce. In the south, villages consisting of a few to several isolated households but tending to be less aggregated are situated near bush islands where gardens/farms are located. Although settlements are adjacent to the forest, most are found several kilometers from residences. The rainy season generally impacts all groups, but peoples of the south are particularly affected by the seasonal flooding of the savannahs. The rains, however, insure the migration of large freshwater fishes into the streams and rivers of the savannah and their being sequestered in shallow ponds for extended periods when rainfall lessens at the beginning of the dry season.

IV. Guyana Chronologies

Though scattered lithic finds imply an earlier presence of hunter-gatherers, chronologies of Guyana prehistory have been based upon seriated ceramic sequences (e.g., Evans and Meggers 1960), which represent relatively recent occupations by pottery-making horticulturalists (cf. Evans and Meggers 1960). The advent of radiocarbon dating (see e.g., Williams, 1981, 1998, 2004) has permitted identifying preceramic occupations as early as ca. 7300 B.P. in Northwestern Guyana. Presently, and in this discussion, the seriated and radiocarbon sequences are combined where possible. In the context of new discoveries and recent radiocarbon dates, the prehistory of Guyana may be broadly divided into three major periods. The first, dating from at least 12,000 years ago and perhaps much earlier, is the Paleo-Indian period associated with the end of the last great Ice Age and the hunting of large animals such as the giant ground sloth. During this time early peoples appear to have intruded into and through southern Guyana as they moved into northeastern Brazil. Little is known of these peoples except that they produced well-crafted triangular-bladed projectiles sometimes made from quartz. As modern conditions appeared some 7,000 years ago, the second period associated with the first Meso-Indian or Archaic hunter-gatherers appeared on the northwest coastland and in the Rupununi savannah.

On the coast and around the swamps of the northwest and Pomeroon areas, numerous shell middens reflect the extensive use of a variety of shellfish. Reflecting this use, Williams (1998) has defined for the Western Guiana Littoral an Archaic Tradition (7330-3550 B.P.), which he divides into Early, Middle, and Late Archaic Periods that correlate with environmental changes.

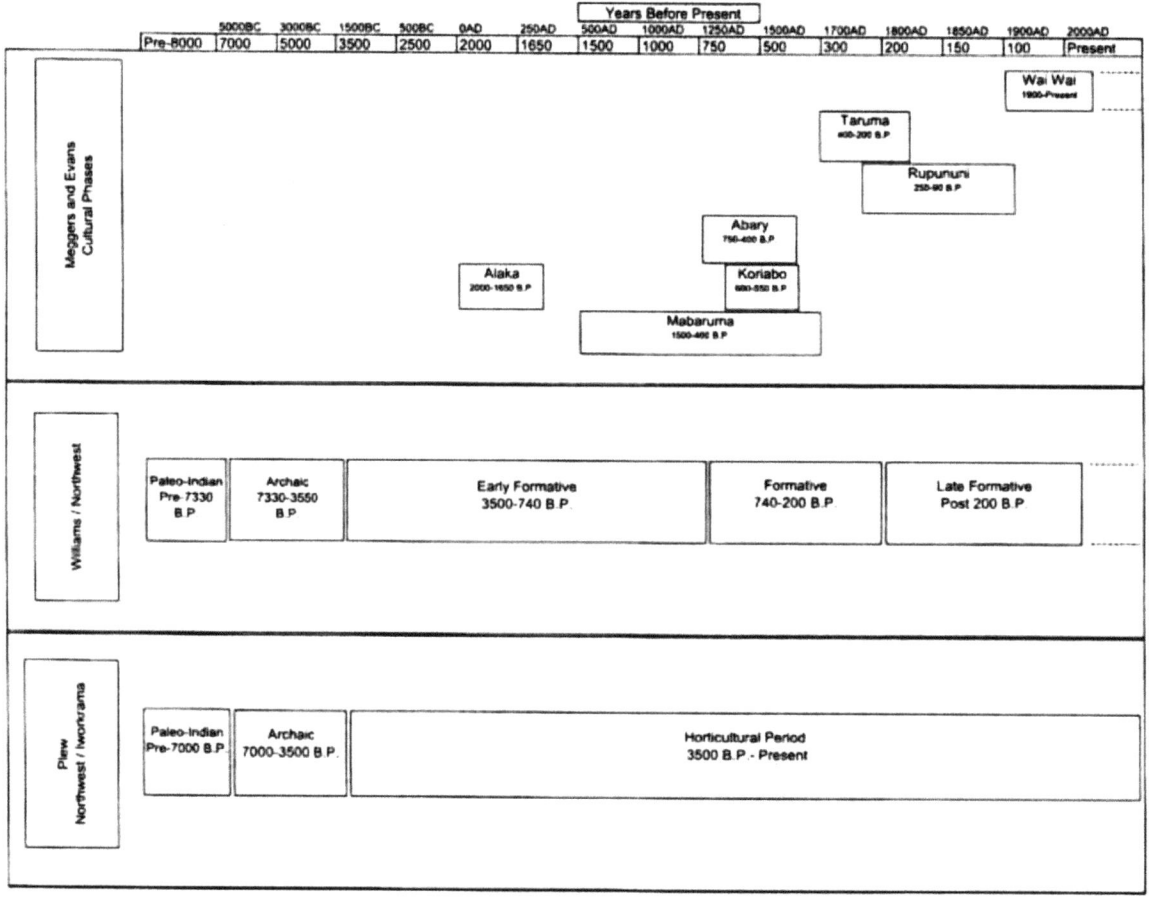

Figure 3. Major Archaeological Phases of Guyana (after Evans and Meggers 1960; Williams 1998)

As a hallmark of this Archaic period, multiple resource use becomes increasingly common and includes the use of "niche" sources, specifically starchy plants. A variety of plants were used for food and construction materials. Because the Archaic period reflects considerable use of the forest, a range of new "groundstone" tools including axes, adzes, and other woodworking and plant processing tools appears in the archaeological record for the first time. In the Rupununi area, various additional resources were seasonally available within microenvironments. Particularly important were the seasonal fish resources of the savannah. Archaic peoples also exhibited an interest in art as indicated by their production of both petroglyphic and pictographic rock art throughout Guyana. It appears as well that peoples began the practice of preferential treatment of the dead. At the Barabina shell mound in the northwest, individuals were interred in flexed positions and with grave goods. In the south savannahs, people were buried in a variety of contexts, including burial urns and cairns. The final period in Guyanese prehistory is the so-called Neo-Indian period or Horticultural period. Beginning around 3500 years ago, peoples in the northwest, the Pomeroon, and the coastal hinterland began to cultivate several varieties of wild manioca. Many of the best known archaeological sites in Guyana date from this period and include Barabina, Hosororo, Kumaka, and Mabaruma on the north coast, at Tiger Island on the Abary, Kibileri on the Mahaica, and Seba on the Demerara. During the horticultural period, populations became increasingly sedentary and began to produce a broad range of polychrome ceramics and griddles used in processing and preparing manioca. Williams (1998:32-34) divides the Formative of the western Littoral into Early Formative (3550-740 B.P.), Formative (740-200 B.P.), and Late Formative (post 200 B.P.) based on paleo-environmental changes and a limited number of radiocarbon dates. Problematic are the limited radiocarbon dates for Guyanese sites (see Table 1). Presently, only twenty sites have been radiocarbon dated and fewer formally reported with contextual data including provenience. The majority of dated sites are Archaic shell mounds in the Northwest. Hence the majority of occupations are based on ceramic seriations. At present, only the simplest longer chronology is emerging. Until many more sites are radiometrically dated, the broader chronology will remain tentative. Most likely, Archaic and Horticultural developments will be found to vary greatly by sub-area.

Site	Site Type	C^{14} Date	Lab Number	Provenience	Reference
Akawabi	Mound	4020 +/- 80 BP	Beta 32187		Williams n.d.
Barabina	Mound	4115 +/- 50 BP	SI 4332		Williams, 1996, 1998
		5965 +/- 50 BP	SI 4333		
		6885 +/- 85 BP	SI 5075		
Haimarakabra	Shell Mound	5250 +/- 30 BP	Beta 51590		Williams 2004
Hosororo Creek	Shell Mound	2660 +/- 45 BP	SI 6636	35 cm	Williams 1998
		3185 +/- 65 BP	SI 6635	20 cm	
		3350 +/- 50 BP	SI 6637	50 cm	
		3550 +/- 65 BP	Beta 20007	20 cm	
		3975 +/- 45 BP	SI 6638	105 cm	
Koriabo	Mound	5710 +/- 80 BP	Beta 27256	200 cm	Williams 2004
		6520 +/- BP	Beta 27057	300 cm	
Piraka	Mound	7280 +/- 100 BP	Beta 27055		Williams 2004
Kabakaburi	Shell Mound	5340 +/- 100 BP	Beta 32188		Williams 2004
Hobodiah	Mound	139 +/- 60 BP	Beta 109244		Williams 1998
Kurupukari	Horticultural	2660 +/- 70 BP	Beta 76247	60-70 cm	Williams 1994
		2910 +/- 80 BP	Beta 76854	45-60 cm	
Waiwaru Market	Horticultural	2150 +/- 70 BP	Beta 27649		Williams 2004
Orella	Quarry	1080 +/- 60 BP	Beta 41949		Williams 2004
Quartz Island	Quarry	2030 +/- 60 BP	Beta 109244		Williams 1998

Table 1: Radiocarbon Dates for Guyana Archaeological Sites*

*This compilation includes dates for archaeological sites only. Hence Seba Creek, often cited in discussions of the archaeology of the Northwest, is not included.

Figure 4. Radiocarbon Dated Sites: 1, Akawabi; 2, Barabina; 3, Haimarakabra; 4, Horsorro; 5, Koriabo; 6, Pirika; 7, Kabakaburi; 8, Kurupukari; 9, Waiwaru Market; 10, Orrella; 11, Quartz Island

V. Pleistocene-Holocene Environmental Change

The early peopling of northeastern South America and Guyana can only be understood in the context of Pleistocene and later Holocene environmental change since it provides a broad context within which to reconstruct the nature of resources available to early populations, particularly in areas where modern conditions do not reflect earlier potentials. Though paleo-environmental data for northeastern South America are not extensive, a number of studies allow for construction of major episodes of change relating to both coastal (littoral) and interior portions of Guyana. During Pleistocene glacial advances, the Guyana coast lay in excess of 100 kilometers seaward from its present configuration. During the Late Pleistocene-Early Holocene (10,000-7200 B.P.), the coastline was progressively inundated by waters associated with the glacial recessions, that left the coastline lying some meters below the present surface (see van der Hammen 1963, Van Andal 1967). After 7200 B.P., coastal conditions favored the development of mangrove swamps and associated peat formation creating brackish conditions prevalent today in areas of the north littoral. Peat deposition is well documented by excavations at Seba Creek, a tributary of the Mabaruma River (see Figure 5). Williams (2004) suggests that between 6,000 and 4,000 years ago, highland runoff converted inter-tidal mudflats to seasonally inundated savannahs. Following a warming interval around 4,000 B.P., water salinity increased and peat deposition ended, creating essentially modern conditions. One of the significant features of the Holocene environments of the coast is the increase in shellfish resources, which Williams (1985b) considers important in the emergence of Archaic culture in the northwest.

This use is correlated with episodes of the alternating presence of freshwater and of brackish swamps, which Williams believes provided an important alternative to use of the *terra firma*. The varied micro-niches of the context are suggested by the pollen analyses of Seba Creek (Williams 1985b).

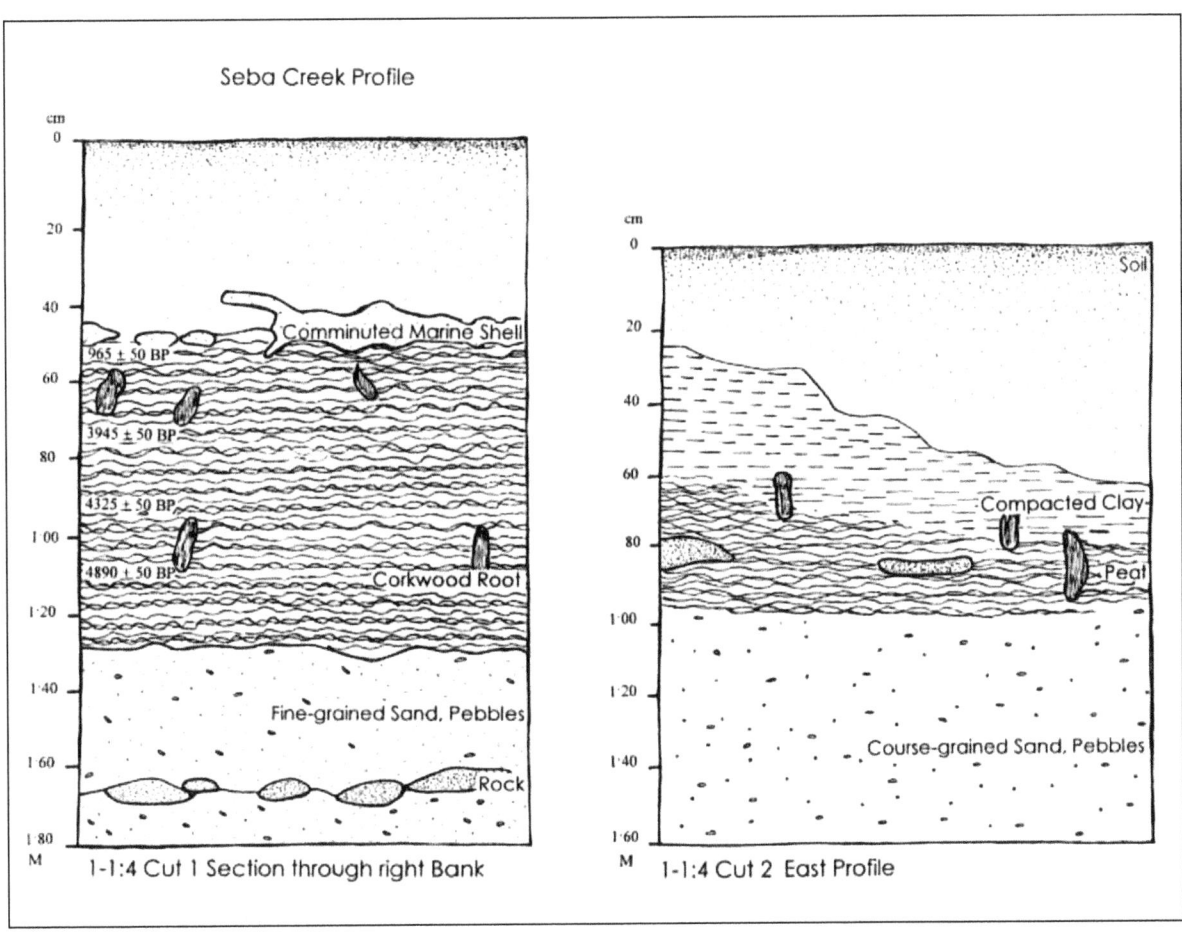

Figure 5. Seba Creek Profile (after Williams 1985b)

The interior forests and savannahs of Guyana have been significantly influenced by glacial climates. Though debate continues about the extent of savannahs within the tropical forests (see, e.g., Charles-Dominique, Pierre, et al. 2001; Vacher, Jeremie and Briand 1998), several dry episodes or warmer periods are known. Between 26,000 and 14,000 B.P., relatively cool/dry conditions prevailed across the Guianas. Following this cooler period, conditions 14,000 and 10,000 years ago were somewhat warmer and associated with increased rainfall. The emergent conditions of the Holocene or modern period are characterized by several dry intervals between 11,000 B.P., 9,500 B.P., and around 4,000 B.P. During these times there appears to be increased settlement of the interior forests and savannahs in what Williams (n.d.) views as a shift to horticulture. Following Haffer's (1969) forest fragmentation thesis, Haffer (1982), Brown (1977), Brown and Ab'saber (1979), and Prance (1973, 1982) have argued for the emergence of *refugia*, the largest across southern Guyana to the Pakaraima Mountains. Recently, Van der Hammen and Absy (1994) argue for a Late Pleistocene (22,000-13,000 B.P.) desiccation resulting in the development of a large western Amazonian forest and several smaller forests in the eastern shield. Importantly, the desiccation associated with these models would have resulted in significantly greater areas of savannah or mixed forest/savannah of the type associated with Paleo-Indian occupations elsewhere on the continent (see Meggers and Miller 2003 for summary).

Figure 6. Amazonian refugia (after Meggers 1994)

VI. The Early Peopling of Guyana: The Evidence for Paleo-Indian Hunters

At present the earliest evidence of human occupation in South America is found at sites in northeastern Brazil. Pressure-flaked triangular points, end scrapers, hearths, diverse extinct and modern fauna, and pigments in stratigraphic relation to rock art characterize these assemblages. In addition, Late Pleistocene assemblages dating between 13,500 and 11,800 B.P. in Venezuela and Chile document a range of bifacially prepared projectile series including willow leaf forms similar to the El Jobo type of the Rio Pedregal sequence, contracting stemmed points commonly known as El Inga, and Pali Aike fishtail points and large bifacial stemmed points (see Meggers and Miller 2003).

In general, considerations of early human occupations in South America have largely ignored the Amazonian region. This is based in part upon the longstanding biases of anthropologists and archaeologists regarding the nature of the Amazonian environment. Traditionally viewed as an ecological barrier providing scarce resources, the Amazon Basin was seen as having limited the potential of aboriginal peoples for cultural development. In addition, the commonly held view that the Amazon Basin lacked the necessary lithic sources for tool production conveniently fit the debate regarding Clovis technology. Despite the bias of North American archaeologists, scholars who have recognized the richness of the Amazonian environment and the innovation of technologies adapted to the utilization of arboreal fauna have argued for a cultural pattern co-existing or coeval with the North American pattern (see Bryan 1991).

Between 1988 and 1992, Roosevelt conducted excavations at the site of Pedra Pintada near Monte Alegre. In a recent publication Roosevelt et al. (1996) provides evidence of a pre-Clovis occupation. Based upon 56 radiocarbon dates from carbonized plant remains and 13 TL dates from burned lithics and sediments, Roosevelt documents an impressive series of occupations between 16,000 and 10,200 years ago, many falling between 12,000 and 10,000 years ago, a period contemporary with the North American Clovis. The occupational levels are characterized by bifacial implements, pigments in stratigraphic relation to cave paintings, and a wide variety of plants including fruits, berries, and palm, and faunal remains which include fishes, mollusks, turtles, tortoises, birds, rodents, and small and large game. Roosevelt's work (1995) suggests that some Paleo-Indians were rock-painting, tropical forest river foragers contemporary with North American Paleo-Indian peoples and provides evidence that Paleo-Indians were more complex, widespread, and diverse in their adaptations than formerly believed.

Interestingly, the site does not contain evidence of projectile points of the type associated with what may be Paleo-Indian contexts in the Amazonian area. Meggers and Miller (2003) have recently summarized the distribution of Paleo-Indian sites in the area. Their overview details the presence of large bifacial stemmed points which occur in a variety of forms that include narrow horizontal shoulders and parallel-sided fluted or unfluted stems and barbed shoulders with rounded stems and bases. Among the interesting forms are tanged bifacial points made from quartz and chert from the middle Tapajós River.

Such discoveries have implications for the early prehistory of Guyana since Williams (1985b) earlier suggested that the earliest peoples inhabiting the Rupununi Savannah of southern Guyana were Big Game Hunters of the sort associated with North American temperate climates. This conception follows in part the convention that the Rupununi is a remnant of a larger Pleistocene Savannah extending along the periphery of the Amazon during glacial maximums when the Amazon was substantially smaller than at present and that it served as a corridor through which early peoples migrated into Brazil. Neither technology nor faunal remains are present, which suggests such a mega-faunal pattern (see Williams 1985b:6). Williams (2004:69-70) has more recently noted that the shape and weight of Guiana points makes it unlike that they were used to dispatch large Pleistocene

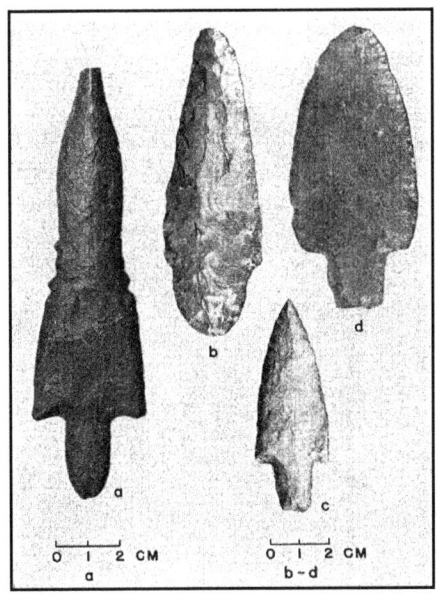

Figure 7. Paleo-Indian Type Points from Guyana (from Evans and Meggers 1960:Plate 8). a, Ireng River, Red Jasper; b, Cuyuni River, Chalcedony; c, Cuyuni River, Chert; d, Cuyuni River, Chalcedony

fauna. The presence of these points does, however, suggest an early occupation of the area. Within the Im Thurn Guyana collections at Cambridge University are three triangular-tanged and bifacially worked projectiles made from quartz crystals and numerous small relatively amorphous chipped stone items which fall within the range of materials typologically characterized by the "Edge Trimmed Tool Tradition" (Hurt 1977; Plew 1997). Two specimens were collected near the Barima River and an additional specimen from the Essequibo River. In addition, Williams (1978, 1985b) reports a similar projectile from near the Ireng River on the northern perimeter of the Rupununi. These projectiles are quite similar to the points from the Tapajós River, identified by Hurt (1960) at Lagoa Santa in Brazil, and at several other locations east of the Andes (see Lynch 1998; Simoes 1976) and most recently near Mariwau in the south Rupununi Savannah (Plew and Pereira 2002).

Summary

The archaeological evidence of a Paleo-Indian presence in Guyana is at present mainly inferred. No formal archaeological sites dating to the period have been found. Most likely the subsistence of early Paleo-Indians reflects a "broad spectrum foraging strategy" in which large animals may have been fortuitously taken but which focused primarily on hunting, fishing, and collecting.

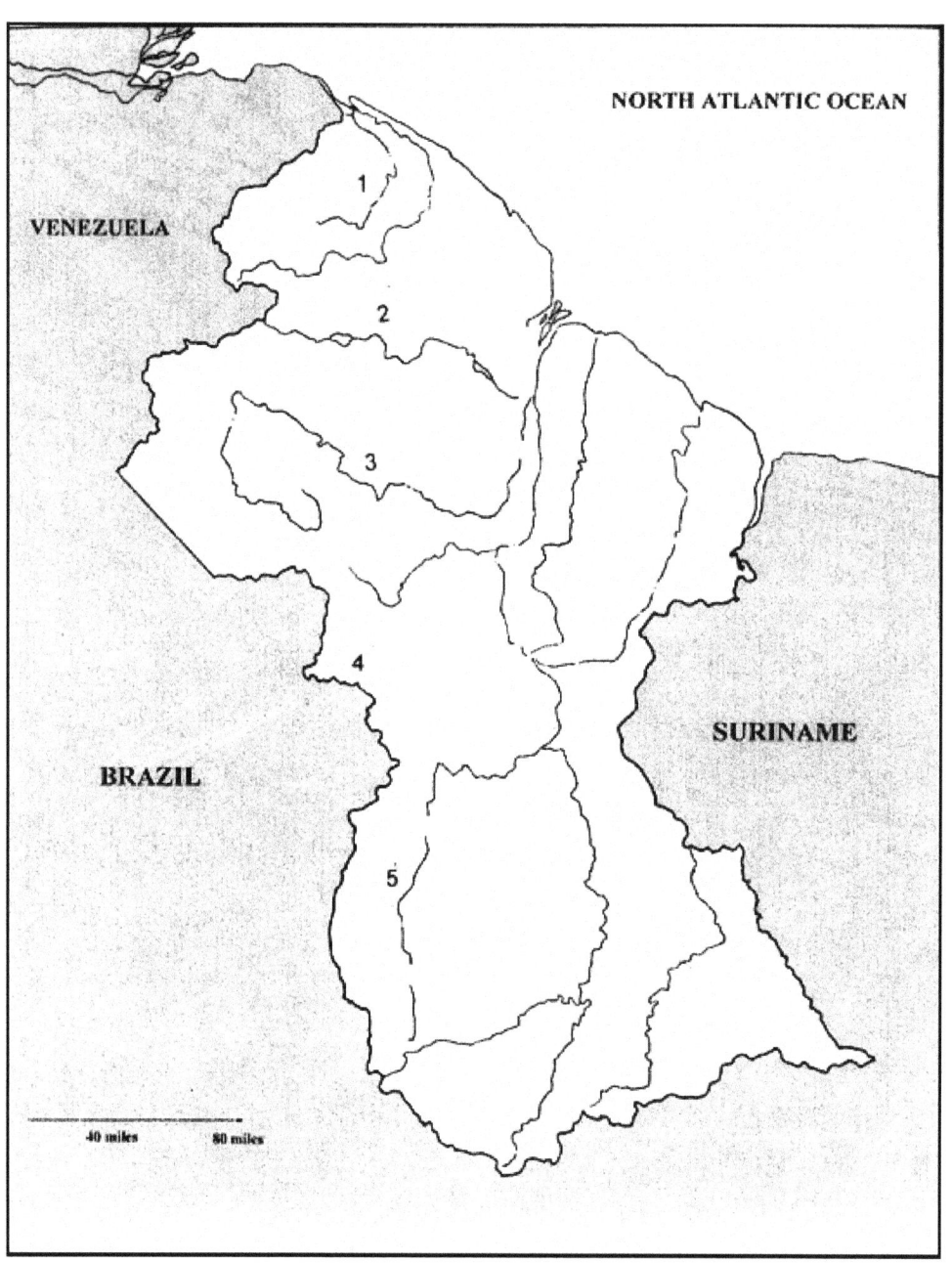

Figure 8. Paleo-Indian Points from Guyana: 1, Barima River; 2, Cuyuni; 3, Mazaruni; 4, Ireng River; 5, Mariwau

VII. The Archaeology of Northwestern Guyana: Archaic Shellfishers and Early Horticulturalists of the Littoral

The past two decades of archaeological research in Amazonia have emphasized to a greater extent than earlier in the century the nature of early human ecologies and the emergence of horticultural patterns throughout the region (Stahl 1994; Versteeg 1985; Williams 1992). At the same time, recent analyses have documented a greater complexity and range of human adaptations than implied by earlier models of Amazonian adaptation (e.g., Meggers 1995; Moran 1993).

In a number of papers Williams (1985b, 1992, 1996) has addressed the emergence of the Archaic Tradition and the beginnings of horticulture in northwest Guyana. He observes the complexity of the littoral ecosystem and notes a number of complex exploitive strategies. In large part, these are based upon ethnographic and historic depictions of resource use for the region. He asserts that adaptation to a complex environment resulted in the development of highly specialized lithic tools that changed little over time (Williams 1985b:22).

As the Formative Mabaruma pattern in the northwest dates relatively late, evaluating the emergence of horticultural strategies that reflect the optimality of resource use by Amerindian populations is essential. Since Williams (1985b) has already demonstrated the nutritional importance of shellfish, future questions may reflect why native peoples shifted their focus from the productive exploitation of such resources to invest in horticulturally based economies and whether this was a relatively uniform development. A further question may address one of the definitive hallmarks of the Formative period, in particular whether pottery occurs much earlier than its presumed appearance and not in the context of a horticultural subsistence pattern. The transition from the Archaic to the pottery-producing horticultural Formative period must also be documented beyond the traditional presence of ceramics, grinding implements and griddle fragments.

Evans and Meggers (1960) described three archaeological phases within Northwestern Guyana: the preceramic Alaka Phase, the ceramic Mabaruma Phase, and the Koriabo Phase, distinguished by geographic location, material culture, and settlement. The Alaka Phase sites, which date between A.D. 1 and 500, are located in or nearby mangrove swamps and consist of small conical shell middens and larger middens measuring up to 80 x 30 m, and between 1 and 15 m in height (Evans and Meggers 1960:63). Subsistence included use of snail, mussel, clam, oyster, conch, crab, bird, mammal, and fish. In addition, sites are often characterized by fire-cracked rock, lithic debris, and ash. Tool assemblages consist of simple percussion implements produced from andesite, quartz, and schist and include in the earlier part of the phase choppers, hammerstones, and picks. Small tools including scrapers were produced from percussion-made flakes. The later part of the phase includes groundstone tools consisting of celts, mortars, manos, pestles, and grinding stones. Though undated, the phase is thought to consist of an early pre-ceramic phase and a later "incipient ceramic" phase in which a few crudely made and shell-tempered sherds of the type Wanaina Plain are occasionally found (Evans and Meggers 1960:63-64). Shell mound/midden sites of the Alaka phase include Kaniaballi, Alaka Creek, and Alaka Island on Warapoco Creek, Hososoro Creek, Barabina, Akawabi, and the Waramuri mound.

The Mabaruma Phase is characterized by sites that vary greatly in their horizontal and vertical dimensions, dating between A.D. 500 and 1600. Habitation sites vary between 900 and 17,500 square meters in area and between 5 and 65 cm in depth (Evans and Meggers 1960:122). It remains unclear whether they reflect a number of short-term occupations over time or larger settlement aggregates. Sites are located above the flood plain and on slopes. Stone tools include choppers, flake blades, hammerstones, possible hoes, manos, metates and polished celts, and a developed ceramic assemblage. Early Mabaruma is characterized by the predominance of sand-tempered Mabaruma Plain which is replaced by sand-tempered Hosororo Plain and mica-tempered Kobarimo Plain in the later part of the phase. Most notable are the Incised and Modeled types, which resemble Barancoid ceramics on the lower Orinoco.

The third phase of the Northwest chronology is the Koriabo Phase, which begins around A.D. 1200 and is associated with large village sites ranging between 1800 and 7400 square meters. The sites, which are rarely more than 30 cm in depth, are typically situated on riverbanks above the flood level. The Koriabo Phase was defined on the basis of three plain and two decorated types. The plain sand-tempered types Koriabo Plain and Warapoco Plain are distinguished by orange and gray cores. A third type, Barima Plain, is cariapé-tempered but occurs in very small quantities. The decorated types include Koriabo Incised, which is executed with sharp v-shaped incisions combined with low appliqué ridges, nubbins, and faces. In contrast, Koriabo Scraped consists of wide shallow incisions produced by a serrated and flat-edged stick combined with low appliqué nubbins and small faces (Evans and Meggers 1960:144-145). Griddle fragments, pot rests, celts, and chisels complete the tool kit. Mabaruma Plain sherds occur in limited frequencies, indicating the contemporaneity of the two phases (Evans and Meggers 1960:145). Hilbert (1982), on the basis of the recovery of Koriabo-like ceramics in the Cuminá region of northeastern Brazil, suggests that Koriabo peoples may have moved into the interior under pressure from European contact. Though the similarity in pottery

Figure 9. Alaka and Mabaruma Phase Sites: 1, Mabaruma; 2, Akawabi, 3, Barabina; 4, Hosororo; 5, Alaka Alaka Creek; 6, Koriabo Point; 7, Waramuri

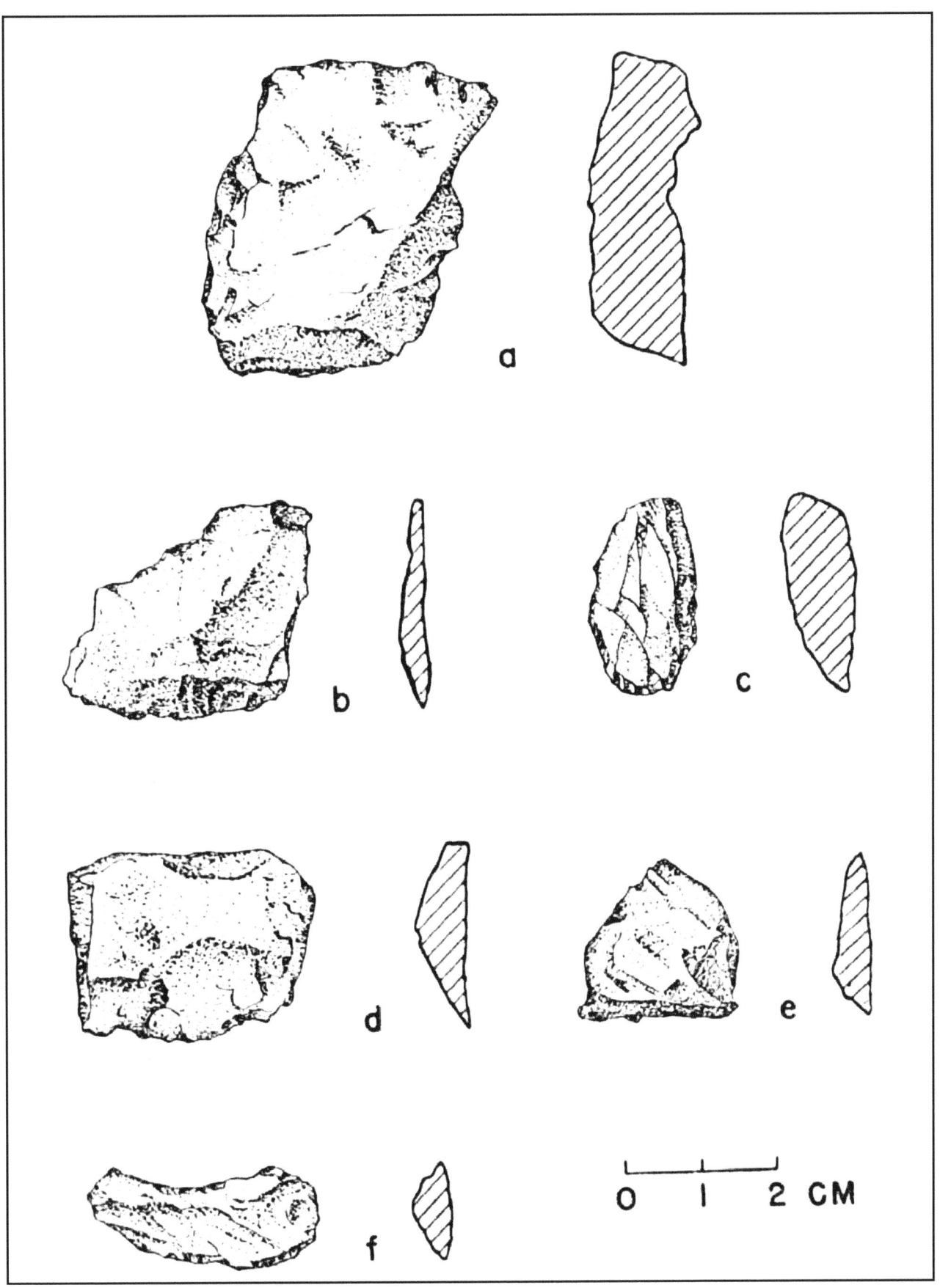

Figure 10. a-f, Scrapers of the Alaka Phase (from Evans and Meggers 1960: 49)

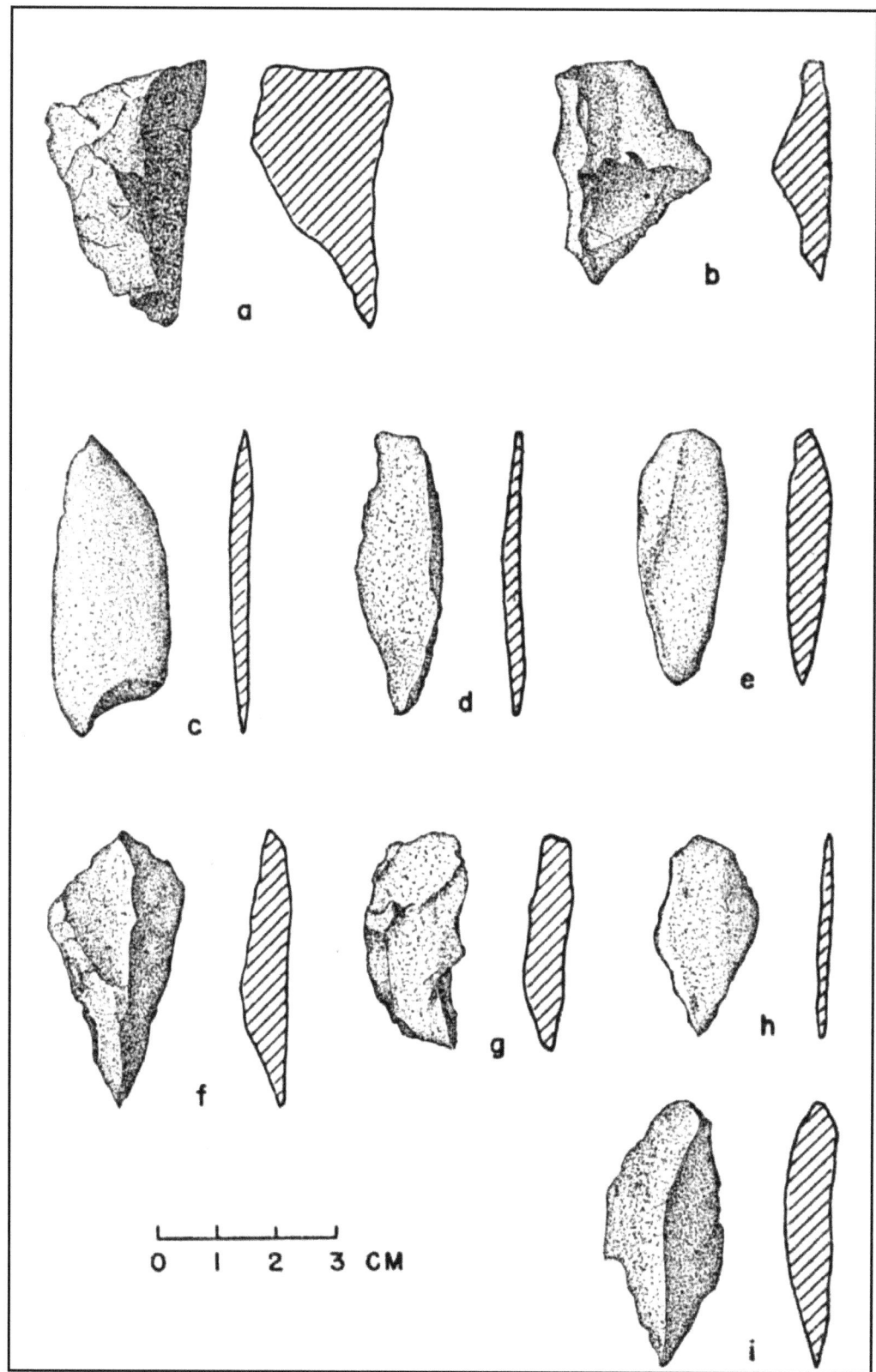

Figure 11. a-j, Alaka Phase Slate Picks (from Meggers and Evans 1960:48)

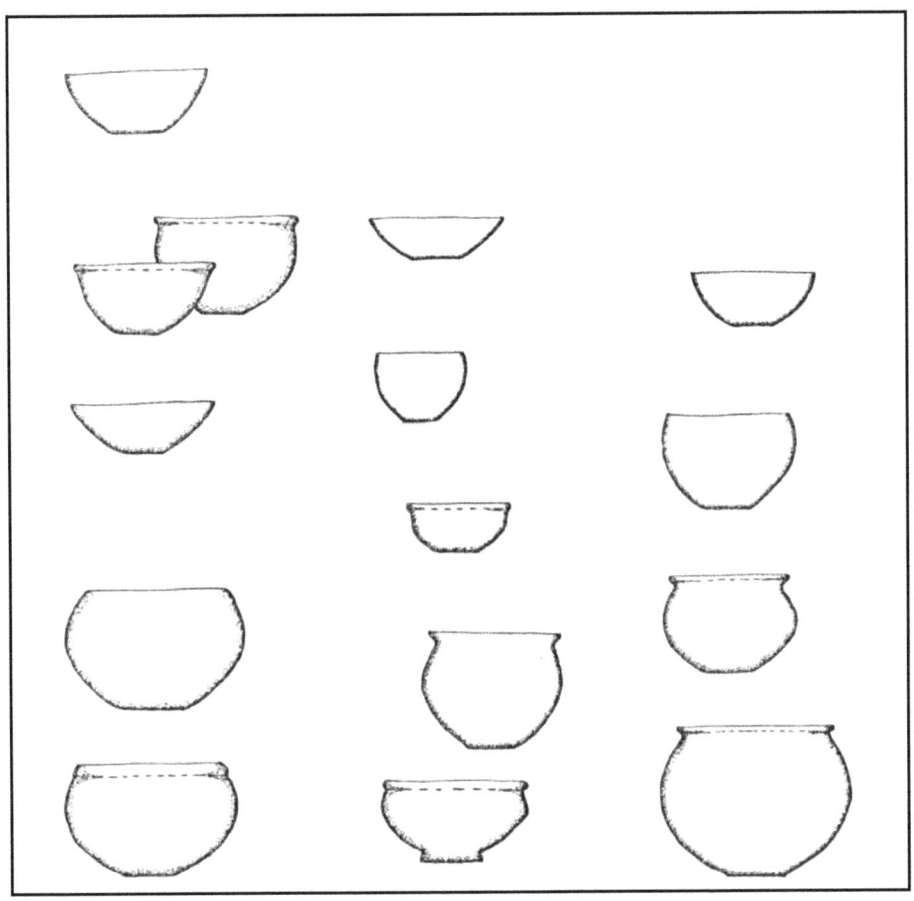

Figure 12. a, Aruka Ceramic Forms; b, Hosororo Ceramic Forms; c, Hotokwai Ceramic Forms (after Evans and Meggers 1960)

is notable, there is no archaeological basis for Koriabo migrations.

The Archaeology of Barabina Shell Mound

Of the shell mounds recorded in the Northwest of Guyana containing evidence of the Alaka and Mabaruma Phases, none is better known or more extensively explored than the mound at Barabina. Williams (1981a:14-15) provides a detailed history of the investigations, which begin in the late 19th century and conclude with his own excavations in the late 1970's. Barabina is one of several shell mounds situated on a series of hills north of the Aruka River. In addition to Barabina, the well-known sites of Hobo, Kumaka, Atapami, Mabaruma, and Seba Creek lie within five kilometers of one another. Located on the west side of Barabina Hill, the site extends over an area of approximately 150 x 300 m (Evans and Meggers 1960:34).

Of the excavations conducted at Barabina, Williams' in 1979 are the most comprehensive and detailed (1981). He excavated three 2 x 2 m test units to sterile sediments at 1.8 m below ground surface. The stratigraphy consisted of alternating levels of shell refuse reflecting different species of mollusks but including the small striped nerite, clams, oysters, crab carapaces, and fish remains intermixed with clayish lateritic soil. The remains of peccary, agouti, turtle, large birds, and cayman were recovered. Subsistence appears to have relied heavily upon the exploitation of mollusk resources associated with relatively brackish environs Williams reports evidence of human remains throughout the deposit (1981:21-22). Radiocarbon dates indicate the deposit accumulated over a period of some 6,000 years (Williams 1992).

The material culture of Barabina includes relatively simple percussion-made stone tools that include split water-worn cobbles, line-sinkers, projectile points and wedges produced from amphibole schist, and small amorphous quartz implements. The chipped stone assemblages affiliate this site with the Alaka Phase. Notably, no shell-tempered pottery was found in the Barabina mound, though a few sherds of the types Hosororo Plain, Aruka and Akawabi Incised, and Akawabi Modeled exhibiting conical punctated nubbins are present on east Barabina and are associated with the later horticultural Mabaruma Phase.

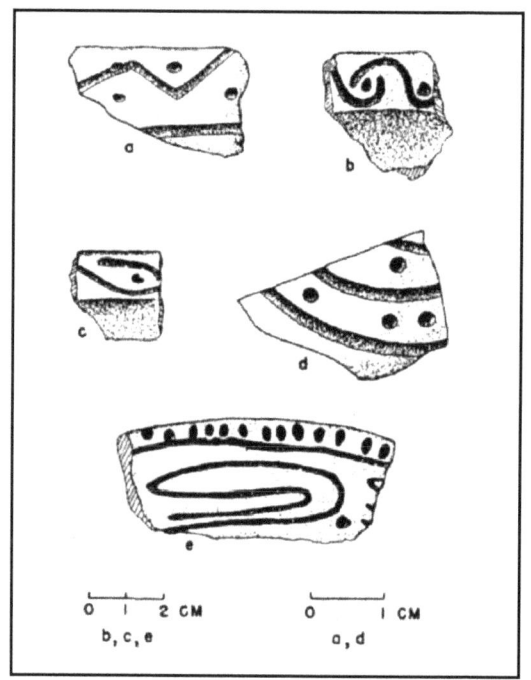

Figure 13. Mabaruma Phase Kaituma Incised and Punctate (from Evans and Meggers 1960:107)

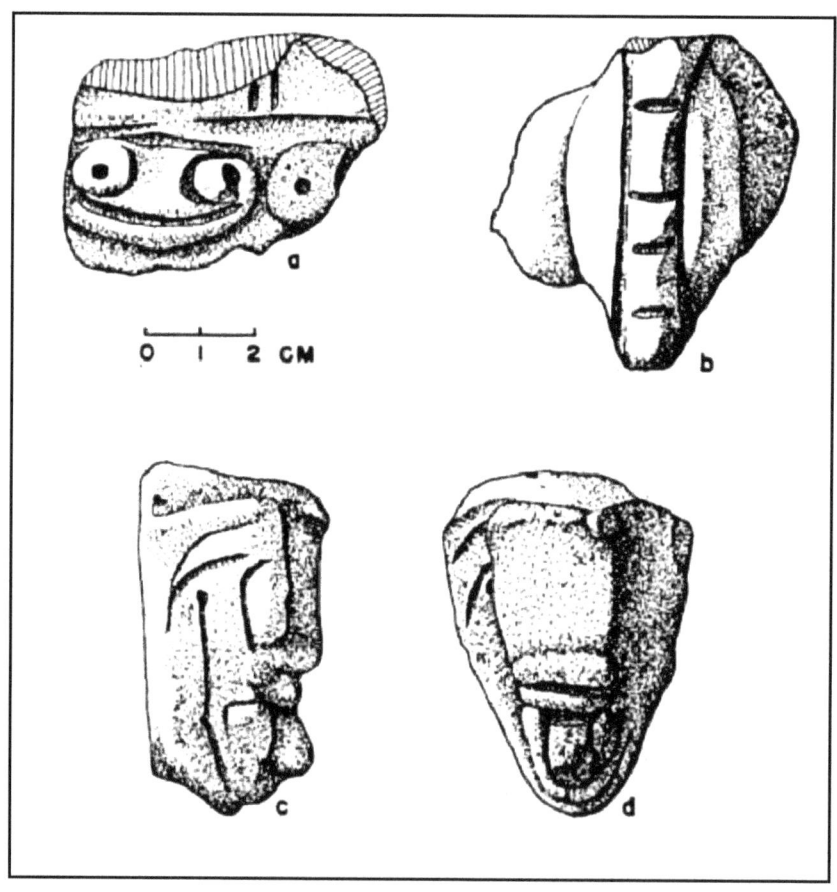

Figure 14. Mabaruma Phase Akawabi Incised and Modeled (From Evans and Meggers 1960:141)

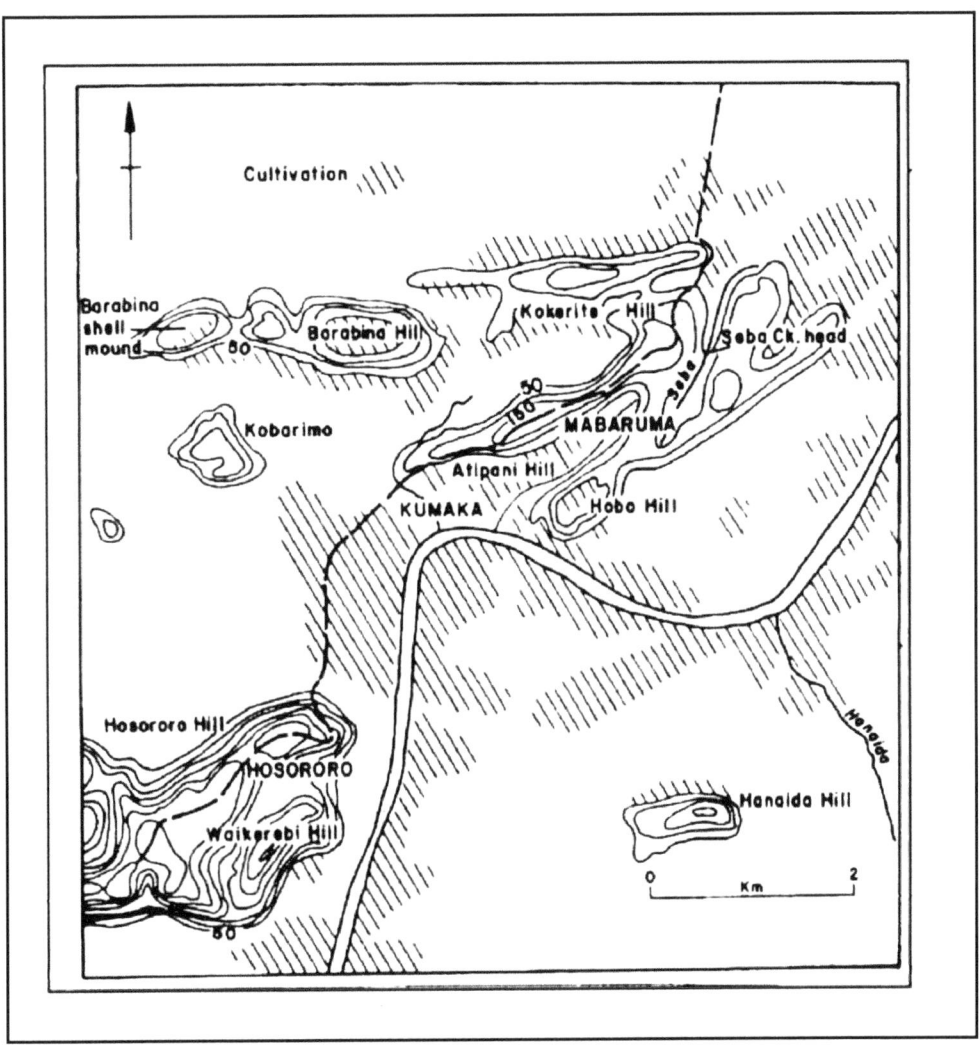

Figure 15. Map Showing Location of Barabina and Other Mounds of the Northwest (From Williams 1981)

(Williams 1981:16, 30-32; Jansma 1981). The site produced evidence of features including hearths, post molds at 1.1 and at 1.40 m below surface, a number of storage pits measuring 30-40 centimeters in diameter and extending to 40-50 centimeters in depth, and five tightly flexed burials of four adults and an infant. In one instance (B-28) a fifteen-centimeter long metal tube (described as steel) of European manufacture is associated with a Koriabo phase sherd.

Horticultural Origins in Northwestern Guyana: A 'Re-Characterization" of the Mabaruma Phase

Williams (1996) posits a "re-characterization" of the Mabaruma phase in which he argues for an *in situ* development of the Mabaruma on the lower Aruka River associated with a Proto-Maipuran Arawak intrusion around 1,600 B.CA. He argues for three periods of development, which include an Early Formative culture dating between 1,600 B.CA. and ca. A.D. 500, a Classic Mabaruma period between A.D. 500-700 and A.D., 1,000, and a Late Mabaruma period dating A.D. 1,000-1,600. The early period is characterized by broad line incising characteristic of the Incised and Modeled Traditions, whereas the Classic period exhibits evidence of Barrancas Incised and Barrancas Modeled Incised. Late Mabaruma is characterized by the appearance and predominance of Apostederan ceramics, which combine elements of Araquinoid and Barrancoid ceramics.

Williams' (1997a) recent conclusions suggest that pottery was produced in a time frame somewhat earlier than estimated by Evans and Meggers (1960:334). His reconfiguration of the Mabaruma phase suggests the possibility of an earlier emergence of horticulture than has been traditionally accepted. While these questions are intriguing and suggest the possibility of early pottery and horticulture in the Northwest, Williams' arguments are largely at the present time assertive and remain to be demonstrated by evidence acquired from other sites.

Level	Fish	Crab	Oyster	Clam	Rock shell	Mussel	Conch
16 - 40	81	6	144	25	13		
40 - 60	695		96	17			
60 - 80	462	12	252	50	12	5	126
80 - 100	546		184	34			
100 - 110	933	16	784	29	4	16	12
110 - 120	Sterile						
120 - 140	966	44	326	98	42	4	

Table 2. Barabina Shell Mound. Unit 4: Fish and Shellfish Remains/Level (g)

Level (cm)	Burial no.	Flexed l	Flexed r	Tightly flexed l	Tightly flexed r	Semi-flexed l	Semi-flexed r	Orientation
40-60	B – 22					150°	150°	280°
60-80	B - 07							disturbed
	B - 13					90°	180°	270°
	B - 23					60°	170°	270°
	B - 27					140°	140°	287°
	B - 34	30°				140°	140°	40°
	B - 37							
	B - 38					125°	90°	55°
	B - 42							280°
	B - 43	85°	90°					269°
	B - 55						180°	270°
	B - 56					120°	80°	265°
	B - 57					130°	70°	270°
	B - 65					170°		245°
	B – 69					120°	120°	270°
80-100	B - 01			10°	10°			210°
	B – 36	20°	30°					270°
						90°	180°	360°
100-150	B - 02	50°	30°					270°
	B - 03	60°				130°		225°
	B - 04							300°
	B - 16	10°	90°					130°
	B - 26							bone bundle
	B - 30							360°
	B - 39							268°
	B – 80							head burial

Table 3. Barabina Shell Mound, Burial Frequencies; Upper Limb Flexture/Level; Orientation

Excavations at Hosororo Creek

Excavations at Hosororo Creek (Williams 1992) provide evidence of Barancoid tradition pottery in a time frame. Radiocarbon dates and associated cultural materials from two trenches indicate that the majority of pottery may be from pre-4,000 B.P. levels (Williams 1997:345). Indeed, the greater number of sherds (N=373 vs. N=218) was recovered between 60-110 cm in what appear to be Alaka Phase levels.

Though Roosevelt (1997a) in an exchange with Williams(1997) argues that the Alaka phase ceramics were recovered from much deeper levels of the deposit and appear to be much older, perhaps dating to the fifth millennium, they temporally overlap the presence of shell and sand-tempered pottery from Pedra Pintada (Roosevelt 1997a:359). Notably, however, the early presence of ceramics at Hosororo Creek may indicate the existence of early Archaic/Formative pottery mounds in northern Guyana (see Table 4). While much work remains to be done before these issues are resolved, Williams' (1996) recent work establishes a foundation for the exploration of the Formative history of the Guyana coast.

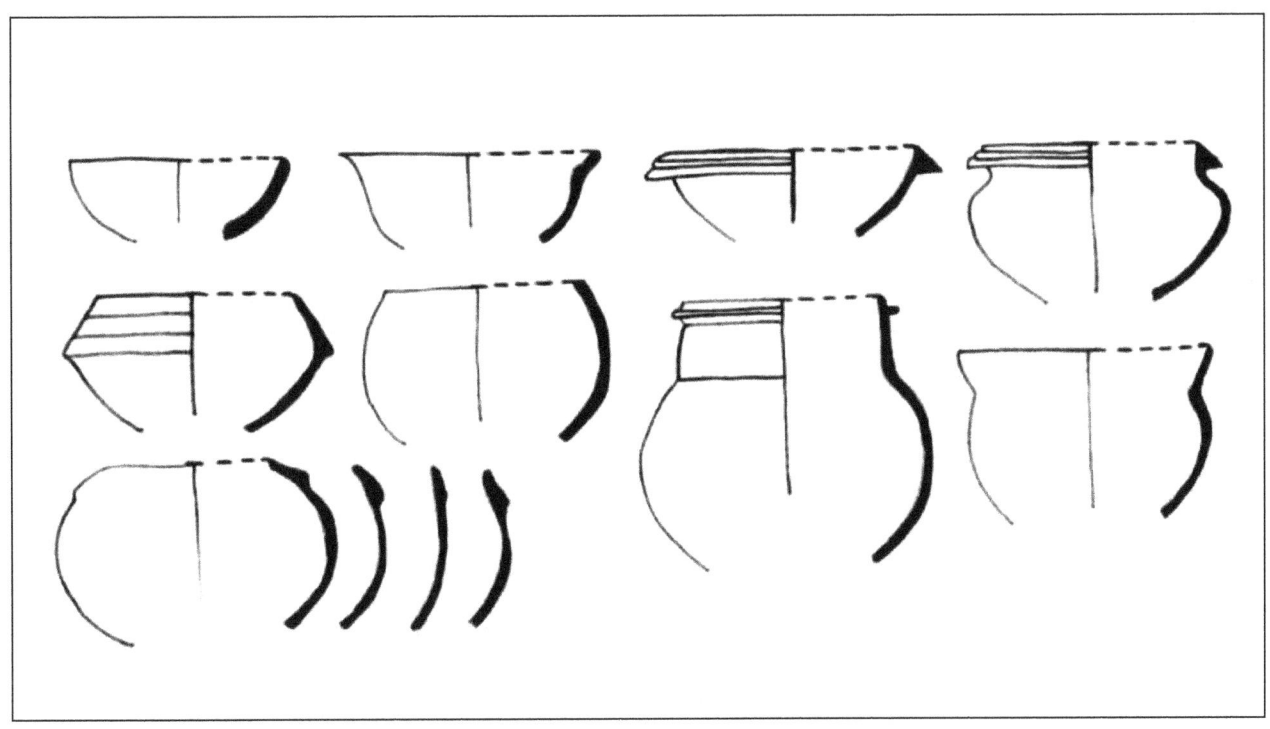

Figure 16. Early Formative Vessel Forms from Hosororo Creek (after Williams 2004)

		Tiestos	*Repercutor*	*Choppers*	*Cuña*	*Piedra para calentar*	*Pesa de línea*	*Quiebra coco*	*Punta de proyectil*	*Formón*	*Metalete*	*Azuela*	*Perforador*	*Hacha*
MABABARUMA	0-10 cm													
	10-20 cm										1			
	20-30 cm	18							1					
	30-40 cm	50			1									
	40-50 cm	50		1							1			
	50-60 cm	100			1									1
ALAKA	60-70 cm	112	1		3									1
	70-80 cm	112		1	1	4	1		1					
	80-90 cm	125		4		5		1						
	90-100 cm	18		1		1								
	100-110 cm	6		1		1						1		

Table 4. Classification of Excavation Levels According to Phase in Cut 3 at Hosoro Creek (Williams 1992:Table 1)

Summary

In the northwest of Guyana, there are presently no evidences of Paleo-Indian occupations. This may reflect the less than hospitable environment of the coast during the late Pleistocene. The archaeology of the northwest includes Archaic and later Horticultural occupations. The Archaic is characterized by the Alaka Phase dating between A.D. 1 and A.D. 500. The Archaic occupations, which are associated with an extensive exploitation of shellfish, are known from excavations of several shell mounds found within the region. The mounds, which range up to 80 x 30 m and are between 1 and 15 m in height, provide insights regarding the economic and social lifeway of the early littoral pattern. The earliest known shell mound is the Pirika Mound, which has been radiocarbon dated at ca. 7, 280 B.P. (Williams 2004). Subsistence data suggest the periodic use of snail, mussel, oyster, crab, and conch as well as birds, fish, and mammals. Though not directly evidenced in the record, it is presumed that a range of plants, including palm, was utilized by local groups. The toolkit associated with the earliest populations includes simple percussion-made choppers, hammerstones, and picks produced from andesite, quartz, and schist. Associated features of the Alaka Phase culture dating between A.D. 1 and A.D. 500 and well-known from Barabina Mound include fire-cracked rock and concentrations of lithic debris associated with the manufacture of stone tools, hearths, storage pits, post molds, and burials. Evans and Meggers (1960: 63-64) also note what they describe as a late "incipient ceramic" phase associated with a few rather crudely made shell-tempered sherds of the type Wanaina Plain. The "incipient ceramic" period is associated with groundstone tools that include celts, mortars, manos, pestles, and grinding stones. The excavation of flexed burials of adults and children provides some limited insights into the social aspects of Archaic life in northwest Guyana.

The Archaic shell mounds of the Northwest have recently become the focus of a debate regarding the early appearance of pottery in Guyana and thereby an early emergence of horticulture. Traditionally, horticulture was associated with large village sites of the Mabaruma Phase dating between A.D. 500 and A.D. 1600 (Evans and Meggers 1960:122). These sites, which range to more than 17,000 square meters in area, are associated with coarsely tempered Mabaruma Plain and an assemblage that includes manos, metates, polished celts, and possible hoes. Mabaruma pottery is replaced by sand-tempered Hosororo pottery in the later part of the phase. Notably, the appearance of pottery in the archaeological record has been taken to reflect the beginning of the Formative period. Williams (1998) has recently argued for an earlier beginning of the Mabaruma Phase at 1600 B.CA. on the basis of early dates at Barabina and Hosororo. His assertions are, however, discussed by Roosevelt (1997a) who notes inconsistencies in data presentations and points to an early occurrence of pottery in Alaka Phase levels instead of those considered Mabaruma. Though presently unresolved, Williams' data may support the growing evidence for early Archaic pottery in the region.

Overlapping with the Mabaruma Phase is the Koriabo Phase beginning around A.D. 1200. Associated with sites ranging to 7400 square meters in area, the phase is characterized by three plain pottery types distinguished by temper and two decorated types that include incised and scraped decoration with low appliqué, nubbins, and anthropomorphic faces. The material culture includes ceramic pot rests, griddle fragments, celts, and chisels reflecting horticultural activities. It is also contemporary with the Mabaruma Phase, which predates the appearance of the Alaka Phase.

VIII. The Archaeology of the Northeast

The northeastern portion of Guyana is characterized by prehistoric occupations that include two major cultural patterns, the Abary Phase (Evans and Meggers 1960) and the Hertenrits Complex defined in Suriname (Boomert 1980). The Abary Phase is found within the Abary watershed west of the Berbice River. It is dated on the basis of the occurrence of Mabaruma Phase pottery sherds to some time after A.D. 1200. Subsequent excavations at Recht-Door-Zee (Wishart 1982b) have demonstrated possible Koriabo influences in the ceramic inventory and the use of wattle and daub house construction (Wishart 1982a). To the east of the Abary River, the Hertenrits complex is defined primarily from excavations in Suriname (Boomert 1981, Versteeg 1985) and appears to date somewhat earlier than the Abary Phase. Occurring as early as A.D. 600 at the Buckleburg Mound in Suriname, ceramics are notable for the use of kaolin temper derived from the Orealla Cliffs on the left bank of the Corentyne River.

The Abary Phase

Though defined originally on the basis of the excavation of only three sites, the Abary Phase is relatively distinctive. The major excavated sites include Tiger Island, Dr. Ho Landing and Taurakuli, which are located within an area of some thirty linear miles 43-95 kilometers south of the mouth of the river and 5-15 kilometers west of the Berbice River. The sites are typically small but contain up to 50 cm of accumulated refuse that Evans and Meggers (1960:182) consider evidence of a relatively high degree of village permanency, as also indicated by the presence of wattle and daub fragments (see also Wishart 1982a,b).

Over 15,000 pottery sherds were recovered and classified into three major types, including Tiger Island Plain, Tuarakuli Plain and Abary Plain. Tiger Island Plain is cariapé-tempered whereas Taurakuli Plain is tempered with crushed sherds and Abary Plain with sand. Stratigraphically, Tiger Island Plain is the predominant early type, followed by Taurakuli and Abary Plain types. Abary Phase pottery exhibits some incision and modeling using nubbins with punctuates. Groundstone tools include axes, adzes, hammerstones, manos, metates, and rubbing stones.

Dating of the Abary Phase is based in large part on the presence of small quantities of Mabaruma Phase pottery (steatite-tempered Hotokwai Plain) at Abary sites and the presence of Akawabi and Aruka Incised and Modeled pottery at Chateau Margot, Mon Repos (Osgood 1946) and Enmore (Im Thurn 1884). Subsistence is known from both archaeological and ethnographic data (see Williams 2004) and suggests that early occupants of the region utilized a range of resources reflecting the coastal and interior riverine environments and would have used a variety of plants, mammals, fishes, and shellfish. The settlement patterns of the Abary and Hertenrits Phases probably varied seasonally which utilizes both habitation mounds and raised field agriculture within primary and secondary waterways and use of sand reefs, ridges, and artificial mounds (see Boomert 1975, 1981; Im Thurn 1984; Osgood 1946; Parsons and Deneven 1967; Poonai 1962; Roth 1944; Verrill 1918; Verstaag 1983; and Wishart 1982a, 1982b).

Earthen Mounds: Archaeological Evidence of Habitation Mounds and Raised Fields

Artificial habitation mounds and raised fields are present in Northeastern Guyana and in adjacent areas of Suriname as perhaps a part of the Abary Phase. Artificial habitation mounds of the Hertenrits Culture are well exemplified by the Buckleburg 1 and Wageningen-1 mounds reported east of the Cortenyne River in Suriname (Boomert 1980; Verstaag 1985). In the general Abary region, artificial habitation mounds have been reported by Verrill (1918) and more recently by Thompson (1979). Many of the mounds rise 2-2.5 m above the surrounding areas and are quite large, having as in the case of the Buckleburg-1 mound an estimated volume of 100,000 cubic meters. Many of the late Hertenrits mounds are encircled by moat-like water bodies measuring 20-100 m in width (see Williams 2004: 326).

The only well-known example of a probable habitation mound in Guyana is the so-called Joanna Mound on the Canje River (Goodland 1964). This appears to be a late Hertenrits (on the basis of similar pottery types) construction measuring 90 m in maximum diameter and 2.5 m in height and surrounded by a moat-like feature. Associated with many of the mounds are wattle and daub. Though it is not clear why the inhabitants chose to construct habitation mounds, it can be assumed that drainage was a primary factor. Interpretation of the moat-like features remains more problematic.

Raised fields of the type generally described by Parsons and Deneven (1967) are known near historic Fort Nassau on the Berbice River (Simon n.d.). The feature consists of 787 raised field mounds ranging between 1.7 and 0.48 m in height, 4.96 and 8.25 m in length, and 1.7 and 6.9 m in width. Constructed from savannah topsoil, the mounds are generally arranged in a linear configuration but have no material culture associations. The presence of raised fields suggests that in some areas innovative strategies were implemented to fit local conditions and thus may have supported larger aggregates of population than previously thought.

THE ARCHAEOLOGY OF THE NORTHEAST

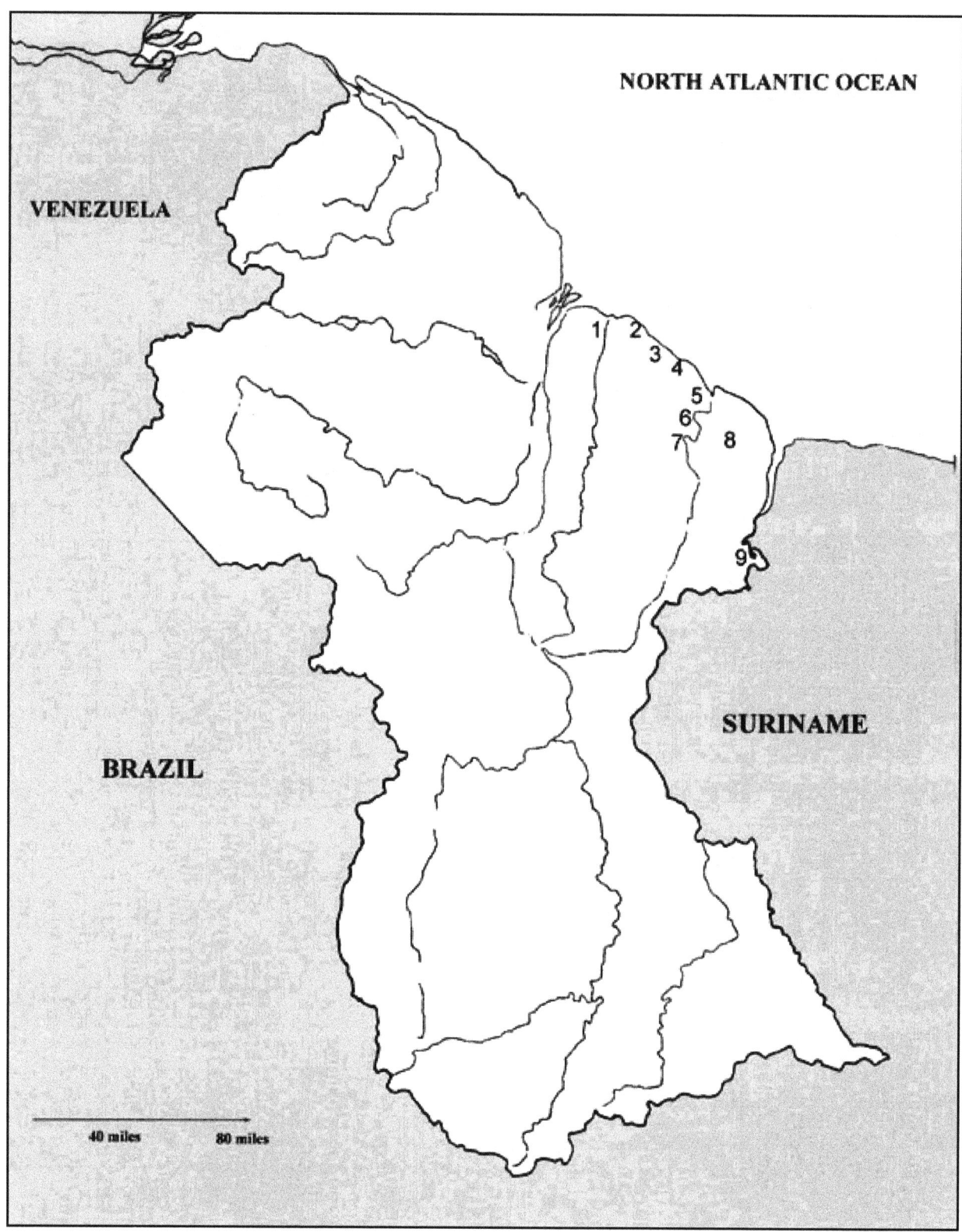

Figure 17. Abary Phase Sites: 1, Recht-Door-Zee; 2, Chateau Margot; 3, Mon Repos; 4, Enmore; 5, Tiger Island, 6, Dr. Ho's Landing,: 7, Taurakuli; 8, Joanna Mound; 9, Orrella

Summary

The archaeology of the Northeastern portion of Guyana is characterized by the Abary Phase defined by Evans and Meggers (1960) and by what appears as Hertenrits culture defined by Boomert in Suriname. The Abary Phase, located within the area of the Abary and Berbice Rivers, is a forest pattern utilizing both interior and coastal resources. The settlement pattern is one in which groups made seasonal use of primary and secondary waterways allowing for the utilization of seasonally varied landscapes and resources. The pottery types Tiger Island, Taurakuli, and Abary Plain succeed one another in predominance within the area and are distinguished by cariapé, sherd, and sand temper. Mabaruma phase ceramics, primarily Hotokwai Plain, establish the contemporaneity of the Abary Phase along with the horticultural Mabaruma of the Northwest. The Hertenrits culture is similar in settlement, subsistence, and material culture to the Abary Phase. Additionally interesting elements of the archaeological record of the Northeast are the presence of habitation mounds and raised fields. Typical of the Hertenrits pattern is the Joanna Mound on the Canje River. Measuring 90 m in diameter and rising some 2.5 m above ground level, the mound is encircled by a moat-like feature. The presence of wattle and daub indicates that these features were habitation mounds. Habitation mounds associated with the raised field features occur in the vicinity of Fort Nassau on the Berbice River. The nearly 800 raised field mounds suggest significant horticultural activity within the area.

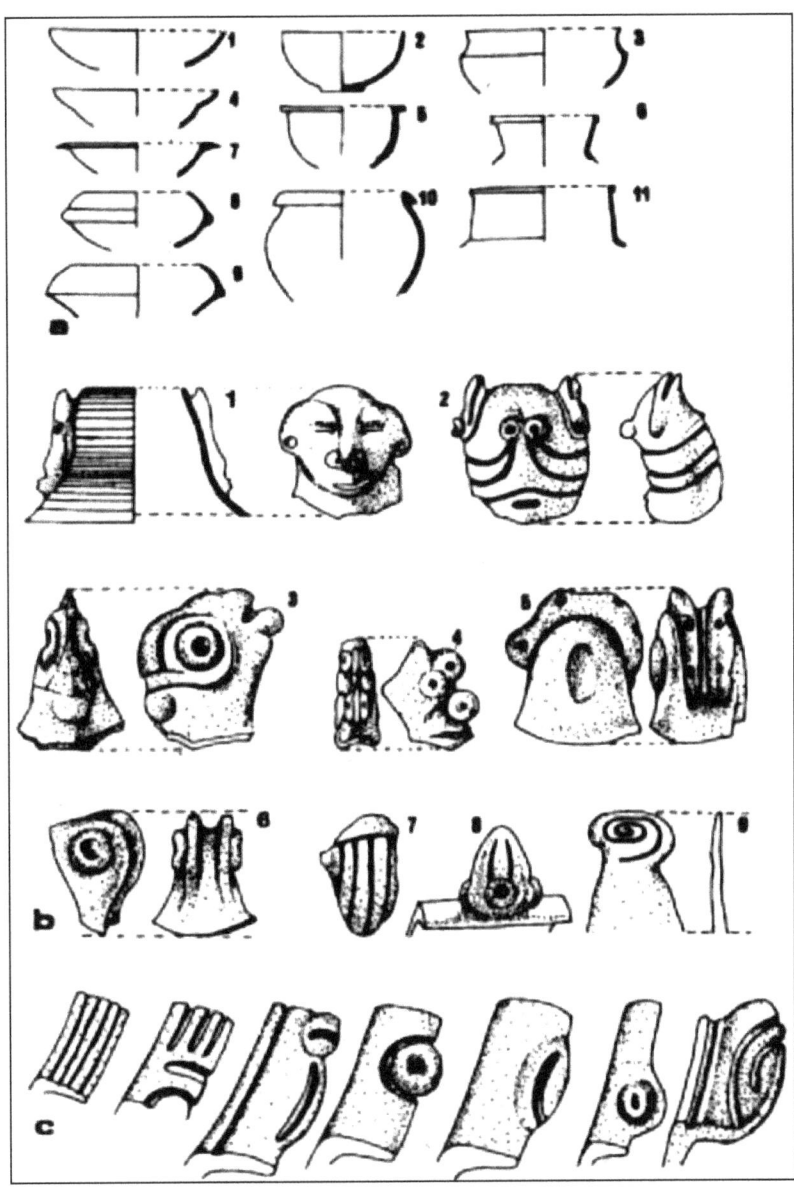

Figure 18. Vessel Forms and Barancoid-Like Adornos from Recht-door-Zee (after Wishart 1982b)

Figure 19. Raised Horticultural Plots on the Berbice-Canje Watershed (from Williams 2004)

IX. The Archaeology of Southeastern Guyana: The Taruma Phase

Perhaps best known of the phases described by Evans and Meggers (1960) is the Taruma Phase of southeastern Guyana. Named after the historic Taruma population that inhabited the area of the upper Essequibo between the mouths of the Kassikaityu and the Kuyuwini Rivers, the archaeological phase is based upon excavations of 24 villages and 11 former field clearings. Sixteen stratigraphic excavations in 11 sites constitute the basis of the definition of a settlement pattern in which sites were located on hilltops and along river terraces having elevations above the flood zone. Sites appear to have been surrounded by garden areas and are characterized by relatively shallow depth of refuse, which in only one instance exceeded 30 cm in depth (Evans and Meggers 1960:245). Refuse depth appears to be correlated with site area. Some sites such as Yochó are relatively small, measuring only 70 by 20 m, while others, such as the Kassikaityu Mouth site, measure in excess of 200 by 100 m. Using seriation techniques and an estimation that a 10% change in sherd frequencies within stratigraphic cuts reflected occupation episodes, Evans and Meggers (1960:240-242) estimated the length of individual occupations and the overall occupation of the area to have been about 200 years. Relative to refuse levels, this suggests that occupations, while repeated in some instances, involved relatively short intervals of time. While sherd frequency variations can be explained in several ways, it appears that the preponderance of evidence supports a chronology of between 200 and 300 years.

In addition to open village sites, petroglyphs documented near the mouth of the Kassikaityu River include both geometric and zoomorphic motifs. Notably absent from the assemblages are burial urns common in other areas. Evans and Meggers (1960:244) attribute this to the ethnographic Taruma practice of cremation. While interred cremated human remains would not preserve in the record, remains preserved in vessels almost certainly would. The practice of placing cremated remains in vessels is known in the Rupununi Phase, suggesting that the absence of burial data for the Taruma Phase may reflect issues of preservation and sampling (see Plew and Pereira 2000). The material culture of the Taruma Phase otherwise consists of stone and ceramic assemblages.

Stone tools include an axe, chopper, rubbing stones, griddle or metate fragments, quartz pebbles, cassava grater chips, and cores and debitage made of chert, quartz, and sandstone, indicating the manufacture of stone tools in Taruma Phase sites. The ceramic assemblage consists of over 14,300 sherds classified into three plain and five decorated types (Evans and Meggers 1960:213). Vessel forms generally include shallow to moderately deep bowls with upcurving walls, direct rims with a variety of lip forms, carinated bowls and globular jars with constricted necks, and everted rims with pointed lips. The major plain pottery types of the Taruma Phase include Yochó Plain tempered with decomposed granite and Kalunye Plain, a fine sand-tempered pottery (see Figure 22). Yochó Plain is the predominant early type in Taruma with Kaluyne Plain becoming the most common type late in the phase. This trend is supported by evidence from three Taruma Phase sites (Muri, Camp Jaguar, and Itabru) excavated by Williams (1978b) in the New River Triangle and the Upper Berbice River areas. A third type, Mawiká Plain, a cariapé-tempered pottery, appears sporadically but is generally somewhat more common during the middle of the phase. Decorated types include Kanashen Incised, Kassakaityu Puntate, Manakakasin Red and Manakakasin Red-on-White, and Onoro Stamped. These types occur with regularity but exhibit no clear-cut trends in frequency. As such they provide little utility in assessing temporal differences (Evans and Meggers 1960:246). In addition to vessels, ceramic artifacts include conical pot rests, disks, spindle whorls, and whistles. While European trade goods are relatively common in many archaeological phases of Guyana, only five Taruma Phase sites produced European materials. On this basis, Evans and Meggers argue for sporadic and superficial contact with Europeans (1960:246). Regardless, the Taruma Phase represents a classical forest pattern.

Williams (1978b) conducted test excavations at the site of Itabru on the Berbice River, recovering Koriabo phase decorated sherds in the earliest levels of the site with mixed Taruma and Koriabo phase materials in the upper levels. On this basis, Boomert (1978) has argued for the possibility of the Koriabo Phase being contemporaneous with early Taruma Phase occupations.

Rock Art of the Kassikaityu: Archaeological Evidence of Fisheries Management?

Evans and Meggers (1960) and Williams (1979a, 1985a) describe a number of petroglyph sites along the Kassikaityu River. Among the elements/styles present, Williams (1985a) describes a number of so-called fish trap petroglyphs that he interprets as reflecting ethnographically known types in the region. These include conical spring, rectangular, cylindrical, and composite types (see Figure 23). He argues that different types of traps were used to exploit various species found within the diverse contexts of rapids, shallows and pools formed along the Kassikaityu and other rivers of the area (1985a). He further suggests that fish populations may have been stratified within some pools and that in some instances pools saw diurnal changes in species. Based on these assumptions Williams argues that fish trap petroglyphs were sign-posted to mark the availability of different species in distinct settings. While the idea of noting locations and indexing species constitutes a novel argument, the consistency of the pattern remains to be

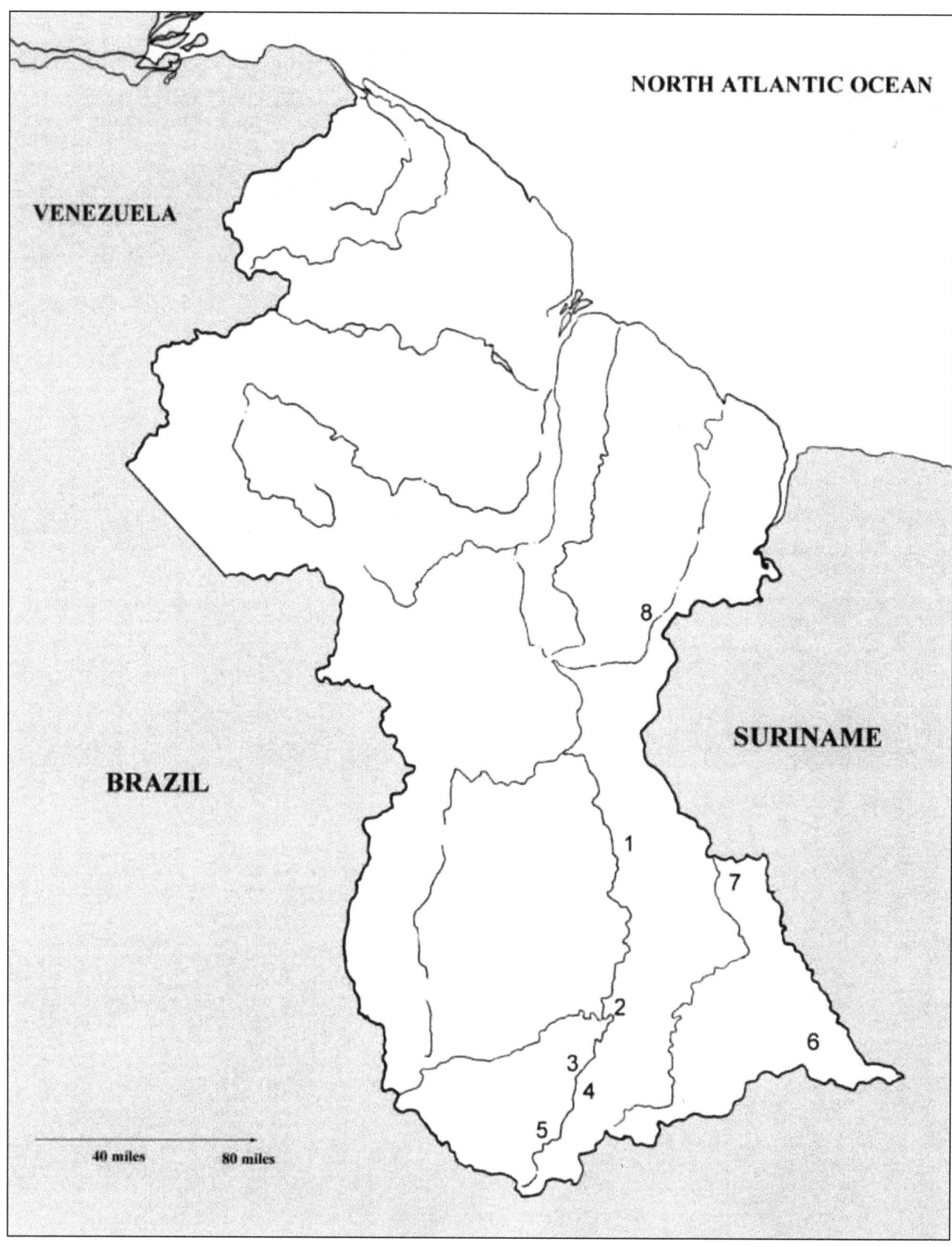

Figure 20. Taruma Phase Sites: 1, Erefoima; 2, Kassikaityu Mouth; 3, Kanashen; 4, Ocho; 5, Kalunye; 6, Muri Mountain; 7, Camp Jaguar; 8, Itabru

documented. Although stratification of species and diurnal species changes have not been corroborated by biological data, Williams' (1985a) observations that petroglyphs and associated grinding surfaces and pollisoirs were manufactured at varying water levels demonstrates the importance of fish in the lifeway of Kassikaityu River peoples.

The Wai-Wai Archaeological Phase

The Wai-Wai are a Carib speaking group known to have moved into the upper Essequibo region following the abandonment of the area by the Taruma. Evans and Meggers (1960) archaeologically investigated two recently abandoned Wai-Wai villages. Their 1952 investigation of these sites was supplemented by observations made in four inhabited villages. These archaeological/ethnoarchaeological observations indicate that small circular and communal pole and thatch of the Wai-Wai from those of the Taruma by the frequency of structures were typically situated above flood level near manioc gardens. They distinguish the settlement patterns village movement. In the case of the Wai-Wai, villages were moved every three to six years and are characterized by shallower deposits of habitation refuse (Evans and Meggers 1960:262).

A collection of 489 sherds upon which the ceramic complex classification associated with the Wai-Wai phase is based includes an undecorated and rather poorly made Erefoimo Plain and two crudely decorated types, Erefoimo Incised and Erofoimo Painted. Plain and decorated forms appear generally to be open jars or bowls with flattened or pedestaled bottoms, rounded shoulders, constricted necks, and everted rims. Erefoimo Incised is decorated with fine to blunt incised lines resembling incisions made in Kanashen Incised of the Taruma Phase (Evans and Meggers 1960:262).

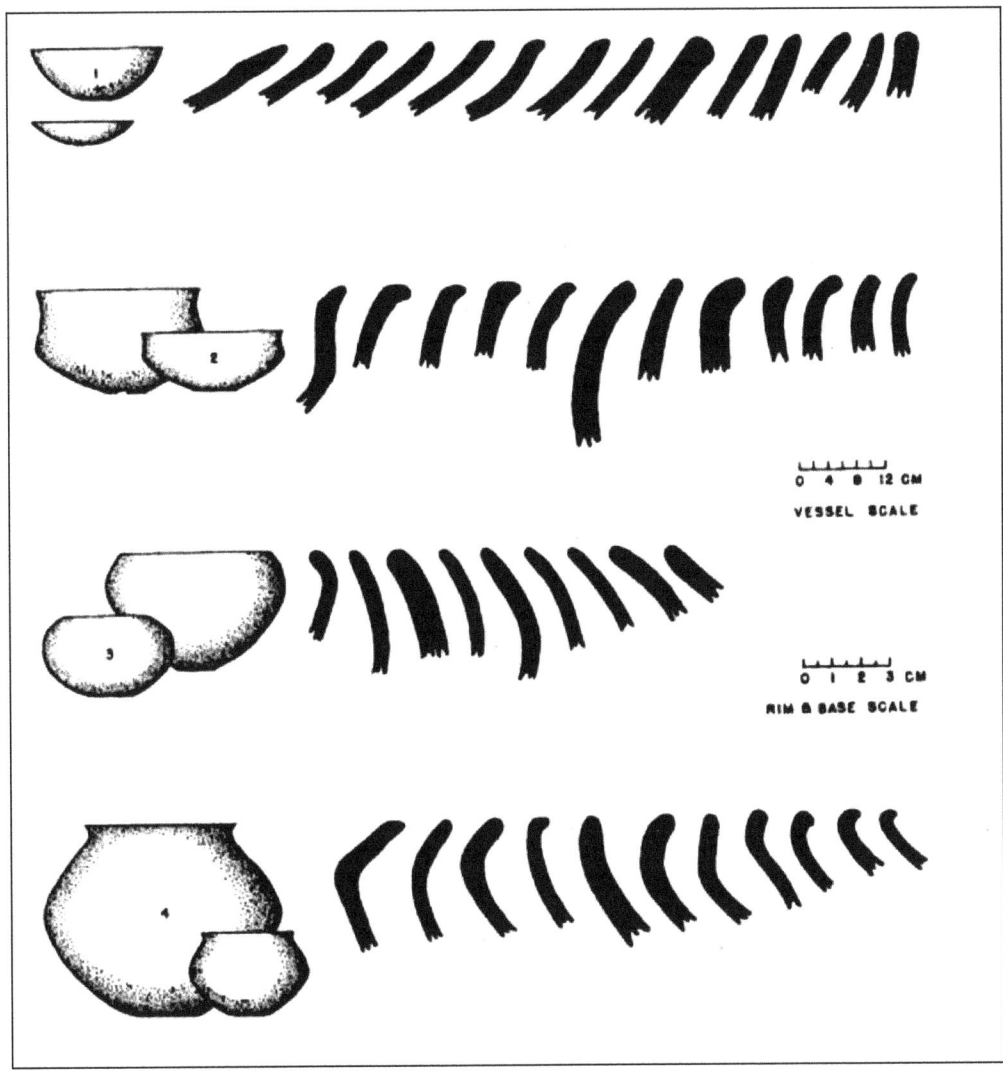

Figure 21. Kalunye Plain Vessel and Rim Forms (from Evans and Meggers 1960:215)

Erefoimo Painted includes zoned parallel lines, zig-zags, diagonal crosshatching within rectangles, and double square spirals represented in black and red. Additional ceramic artifacts include pot rests and thick disk-shaped spindle whorls. Items of European origin include one green glass bottle fragment, a mirror fragment and 1,144 glass seed beads in a variety of colors. In general, the Wai-Wai archaeological phase would appear to reflect the pattern known ethnographically. Notably, late 19th/20th century adaptations of the Wai-Wai to the southeastern Guyana rainforest appear remarkably similar to those of the earlier Taruma Phase, which most probably existed in the area for 100 years prior to the extinction of the Taruma (Evans and Meggers 1960: 268-269) (see Figure 24).

Summary

Southeastern Guyana and adjacent Suriname are characterized by the Taruma archaeological phase. Named for the now extinct ethnographic Taruma population, the phase is known from the Upper Essequibo between the mouths of the Kassikaityu and Kuyuwini Rivers. Sites vary in size and location but are generally associated with shallow refuse and are situated above high water levels. Shallow refuse levels suggest short-term uses of the sites. Material culture includes a wide range of chipped and groundstone tools and debitage suggesting the manufacture of stone tools within villages. The ceramic assemblage includes three plain and five decorated types. Vessel forms include shallow to deep bowls with a variety of lip and rim forms and carinated bowls and globular jars. Plain pottery types include granite-tempered Yoché Plain common in early horizons, sand-tempered Kalunye Plain--the most common type late in the phase--and caraiapé-tempered Mawiká Plain, which occurs sporadically but is generally more common during the middle of the phase. Decorated types, which exhibit no frequency trends, include Kanashsen Incised, Manakakasin Red and Red-on-White, Kassikaityu Punctate, and Onoro Stamped. Ceramic pot rests, whistles, disks, and spindle whorls are common. In contrast to other areas, particularly the Rupununi, European trade goods are relatively rare. Common to the area are numerous rock art sites on and in the vicinity of the Kassikaityu River, occurring along rapids, shallows, and deeper pools. Motifs defined by Williams (1985a) as fish-trap petroglyphs are believed to sign-post the seasonal availability of different species within distinct settings. Finally, Evans and Meggers (1960) have identified a Wai-Wai archaeological phase which is similar to but differs from the preceding Taruma pattern in length of occupation. The phase, which dates from the late 19th to the middle of the 20th century, has been defined on the basis of archaeological excavations and ethnoarchaeological observations of contemporary Wai-Wai villages visited by Evans and Meggers. Material hallmarks include Erefoimo Plain, Incised, and Painted pottery. The incised type resembles Taruma phase Kanashen Incised, while Erefoimo Painted includes parallel zoning, zig-zags, and diagonal crosshatching within rectangles and double squared spirals.

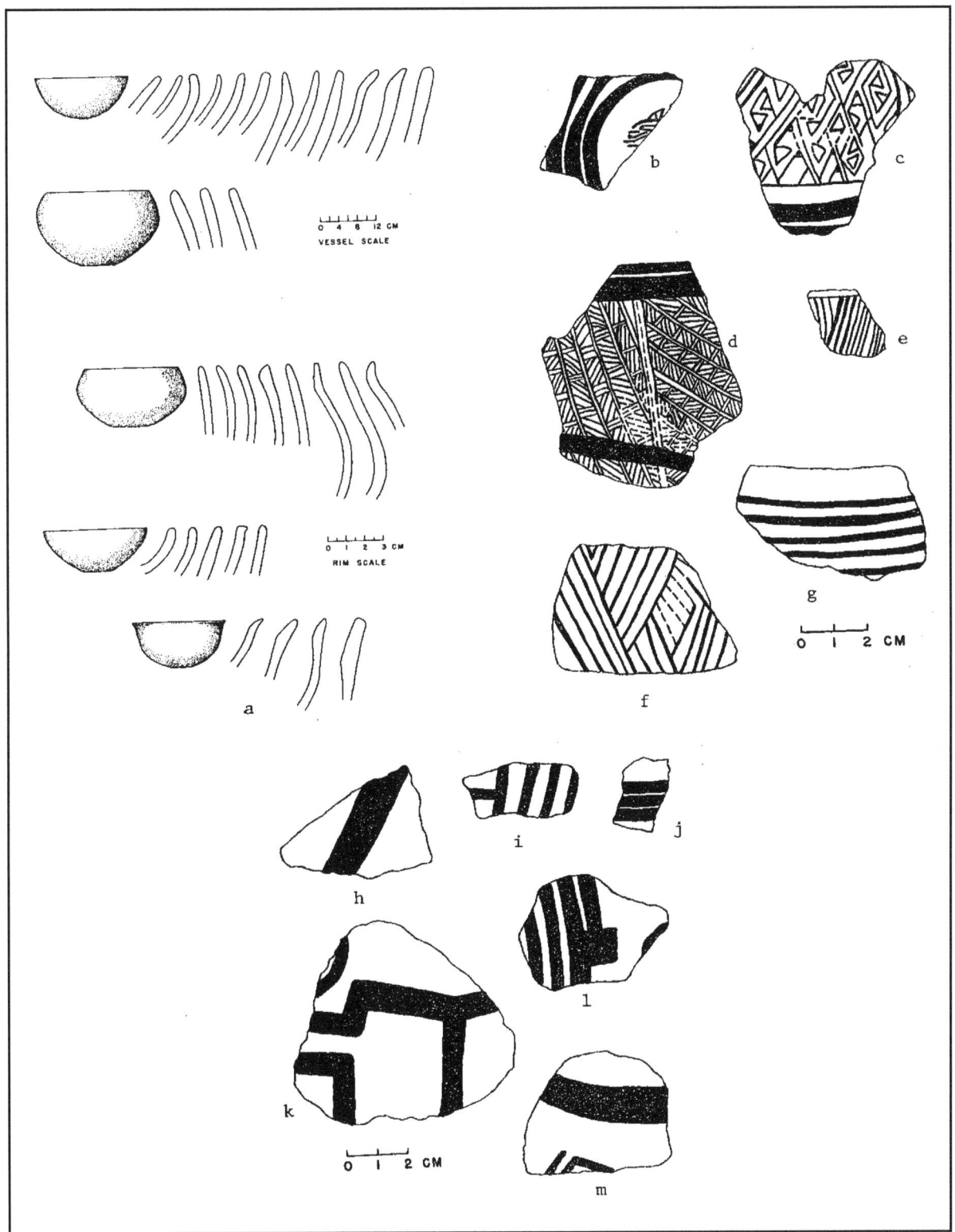

Figure 22. Decorated Pottery of the Taruma Phase, a. Vessel Forms; b-f, Manakashin Red-on-White Fine Line Intricate Patterns; h-m, Manakasin Red-on-White Broad Line Decoration (after Evans and Meggers 1960:222-223)

THE ARCHAEOLOGY OF SOUTHEASTERN GUYANA

Figure 23. Fish Trap Petroglyphs on the Kassikaityu (after Williams 1985a:364).

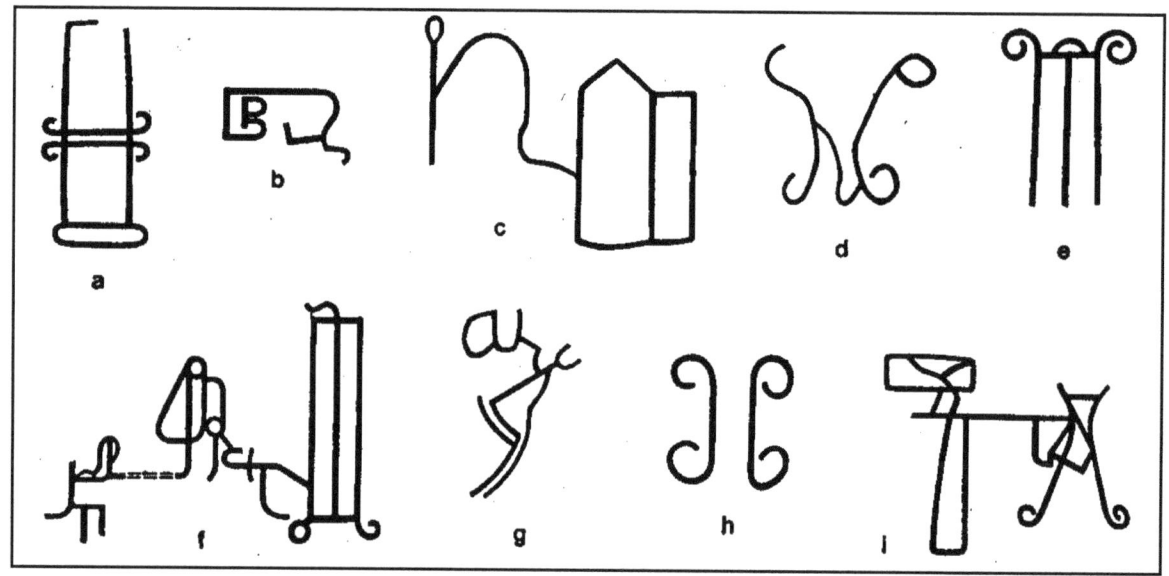

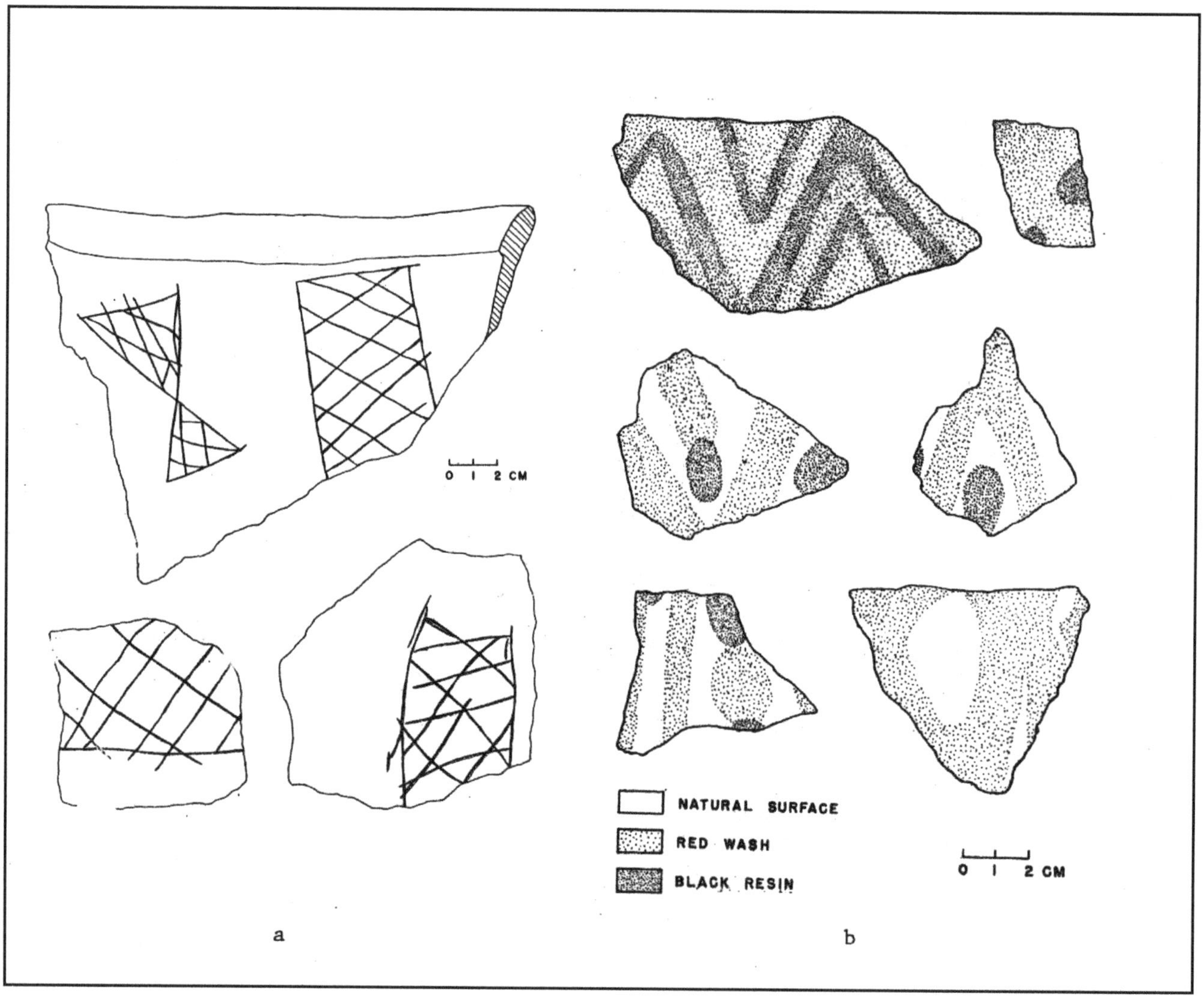

*Figure 24. Wai-Wai Phase Ceramics; a, Erefoimo Incised; b, Erefoimo Painted
(after Evans and Meggers 1960:251-253)*

X. The Archaeology of the Rupununi Savannah

The Rupununi savannah accounts for nearly half the national territory of Guyana (Williams 1979a), yet the archaeology of the area remains relatively unexplored. Developing an understanding of the range of sites and cultural materials involves addressing issues of chronology, material assemblage diversity, and settlement which are unique among the cultural areas of Guyana.

The Paleo-Indian Period

Evidence of the Paleo-Indians in the Rupununi is limited to a few discoveries, including Williams' (1985b) report on a Paleo-like point from the Ireng River. Plew (1997) has identified from the Im Thurn collections at Cambridge University a second triangular quartz specimen, which also came from the Ireng River. An additional specimen from the Mariwau area has been identified (Plew and Saras 2001). At present, these finds constitute the limited record of early Paleo-Indians in the Rupununi (Evans and Meggers 1960, pl. 8).

The Archaic Period

As defined by Williams (1985b), Archaic artifacts, features, and sites in the North Rupununi include chipped and groundstone artifacts (Evans and Meggers 1960; Roth 1924, 1929; Williams 1978; Plew n.d.). Features include rock alignments (Brown 1876; Henderson 1952), rock circles (Brown 1873; Henderson 1952) and rock piles (Henderson 1952), grinding surfaces or depressions, sharpening grooves (*pollisoirs*), and petroglyphs. Earlier explorers noted petroglyphs in the north Savannahs (see Hortsmann and Tollenaer in Harris and de Villiers 1911), while additional glyphs have been described by Brown (1876) on the Kwitaro. Petroglyphs have also been reported by Dubelaar and Berrange (1979), Hanif (1967), Poonai (1970), Goodland (1976), and most notably by Williams (1979a, 1985b) at Aishalton and at Shiriri Mountain (Plew and Pereira 2001). Williams (1985b) considers these features to date to the pre-horticultural Archaic period. It appears likely that many of the Archaic artifacts and features are also associated with later horticultural communities.

The Rock Art of Aishalton

most explorers of the south savannahs, the rock art was only systematically studied in the late 1970's by Denis Williams (1979a). The site area is a relatively open plain adjacent to Makatau Mountain, located on the outskirts of Aishalton Village. Williams identified 30 petroglyph sites consisting of 686 motifs that are inscribed on granite boulders of variable sizes (many as large as two to 2 to 3 m in length) on the savannah and within Makatau Cave on the southern perimeter of Aishalton Mountain (1979a). Among the best known Archaic Period sites in the Rupununi are the rock art sites of Aishalton. Noted by

Petroglyphs consist largely of geometric and bimorphic elements. The manufacture, which may be described as employing a broad line and deep groove (pit and groove) technique, uses numerous dots and furrows in combinations with geometric and bimorphic representations (see Figure 26, Table 5).

Williams (1979a, 1985a) suggests that combinations of punctuates and straight furrows with bimorphic elements, mostly birds and game animals, represent a system of enumeration common among hunter-gatherers throughout the Americas. He is careful to avoid the suggestion that the configurations represent a numerical system but suggests that differing combinations and orientations of motifs indicate the location and range of edible plants and animals and of raw material sources. He argues for a sequential "reading" of the combinations of elements signing the presence of resources in different areas. He observes that subsistence was undoubtedly connected to rituals associated with the *peaiman* or shaman but without suggesting that shamans may have produced the rock art.

An additionally interesting aspect of Williams' (1979a) Aishalton research is the description of stone tools used in the manufacture of rock art. He excavated small trenches along the margins of three petroglyph boulders, recovering a total of 84 stone tools that included scribes (n=33), gouges (n=2), groovers (n=36), and polishers (n=8). Scribes typically possessed sharper edges for cutting while gouges produced punctuates and grooves. So-called groovers consisted of flakes and pebbles showing considerable abrasion at angles as great as 45°. Polishers presumably served as gravure finishing tools.

The majority of tools were produced from granite and quartz. This is the only site in Guyana where a significant tool kit used in manufacture of rock art has been identified and described.

On the basis of comparisons with styles in North America and the Caribbean, Williams (1979a) suggests a time range between 5,000 and 3,000 B.CA., which would place the rock art within the Meso-Indian or Archaic Period. Since there are common motifs throughout southern Guyana, being unable to chronometrically date the rock art of the Rupununi makes it difficult to know with certainty whether all or some of the petroglyphs are attributable to Archaic peoples or whether some, as would seem to be the case with rock art in the area of the Kassikaityu River, are associated with more recent horticultural groups.

THE ARCHAEOLOGY OF THE RUPUNUNI SAVANNAH

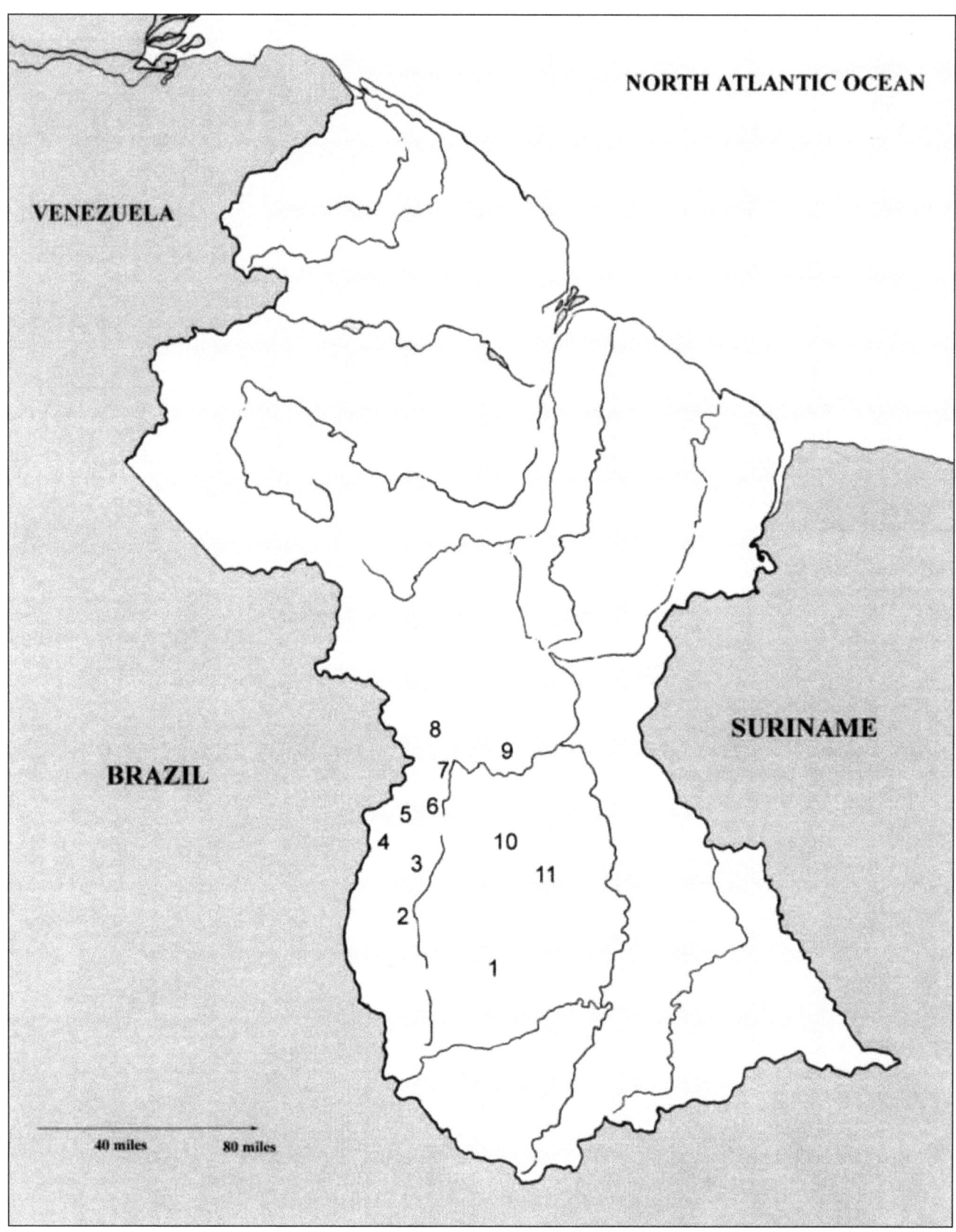

Figure 25. Selected Archaeological Sites of the Rupununi: 1, Aishalton; 2, Shiriri Mountain; 3, Mariwau; 4, Sauriwau; 5, Shulinab; 6, Moco-Moco; 7, Yupukarai; 8, Toka, 9, Annai; 10, Wie Wie Tau; 11, Bei Tau

Figure 26. Granite Boulders near Aishalton

Figure 27. Rock Art Designs on Boulders Near Makatau Cave

The Horticultural Period

The most extensive investigation of the Rupununi conducted by Evans and Meggers (1960) identified a number of site types and pottery forms that serve as the basis for definition of the Rupununi Phase. Two pottery types, Rupununi Plain and Kanuku Plain, account for the majority of ceramics from the area. The seriation of these types suggests an inverse distribution over time. Based on the associated historic items, Evans and Meggers

(1960) concluded that the phase dated from the end of the 18th century. In this regard they viewed settlement of the savannah as a post-European phenomenon (Evans and Meggers (1960:326). Site types include habitation, ceremonial, cemetery, and petroglyph. Habitation sites include open villages as at Moco-Moco near Lethem and the Maubi-Wau villages to the south on the eastern Rupununi. The use of caves and rockshelters for habitation and perhaps for other activities was noted at a number of sites including Wie-Wie-Tau Cave located to the south of Shiriri Mountain. Wie-Wie-Tau represents a common pattern of sparse distribution of materials, consisting primarily of a few sherds and occasional animal remains.

Cemetery sites are quite common in the Rupununi. These consist of caves and rockshelters used for burials and ledges, and walls of granite boulders upon which or adjacent to which burial urns were deposited. The former pattern is well represented by Moco-Moco, Bei-Tau, and Tamrio-Wau shelters, whereas the latter pattern is characteristic of Upper Karakara. In the south Rupununi, ceremonial sites include locations adjacent to granite boulders, where large shallow bowls of the Kanuku Plain type were found. Ceremonial locations, which include Marikanwauda and Mache-En-Tau, are not associated with other materials, though a few white trade beads were found inside the Marikanwauda vessel. To the north in the Annai area, ceremonial sites were reported to include stone alignments of the types described by Brown (1876) and Henderson (1952). Evans and Meggers (1960:300) noted the previous observations of Brown and Henderson but did not locate alignments of this type during their survey.

The material culture of the Rupununi Phase as described by Evans and Meggers (1960) includes a range of chipped and groundstone artifacts made predominately from syenite, quartzite, sandstone, and felsite. These include anvils, grooved axes, choppers, hammerstones, hoes, manos, metates, cores and flakes, and two stone bowl fragments. More prominently represented are pottery vessels and sherds of the types Kanuku and Rupununi Plain. Made by coiling, the pottery is found in a variety of surface colors within a range of orange to reddish orange to reddish brown and is characterized by three forms. These include shallow to deep bowls with out-sloping to almost vertical walls, direct rims and flattened to rounded lips, globular bowls and jars with walls rounded and incurving with rounded lips, and bowls and jars with a ridge of carination forming sharp to rounded shoulders, above which walls incurve before expanding to direct rims having flattened or rounded lips (Evans and Meggers 1960:307-308). Kanuku Plain is distinguished from Rupununi Plain by the absence of a gray core. In addition to a few cariape-tempered sherds, a number of rare decorated sherds were noted. Techniques include incision, applique, punctate, white paint, white slip, and red film. The almost complete absence of decoration in the Rupununi Phase makes these finds particularly notable. Pottery artifacts include three fragments of a pottery rest, crude anthropomorphic figurine fragments, a coiled ceramic disk, nineteen shaft polishers made from both Kanuku and Rupununi Plain sherds and a cubical rubbing tool (Evans and Meggers 1960) (Figure 28).

The Shiriri Mountain Survey

Recent archaeological reconnaissance in the area of Shiriri Mountain identified four additional archaeological sites belonging to the Rupununi Phase (Evans and Meggers 1960). Though no absolute dates were obtained as a result of the findings, Plew and Peirera (2001) follow the presumption of Evans and Meggers (1960) that the Rupununi Phase dates to the Late Prehistoric or Early Historic period. The survey, though limited in scope, identified a greater degree of variation in settlement types. These included a workshop/manufacturing station, a rock alignment, red pictographic rock art, and an unusual cemetery, which produced painted pottery. Though evidence of manufacturing of chipped stone tools is probably represented at locations previously described by Evans and Meggers (1960), site IX-2:77, a small lithic tool manufacturing area appears to be the first such station located away from a habitation site.

Stone Alignments in the Rupununi

Stone alignments are known throughout the area, having been reported by Evans, Meggers and Cruxent (1959) in eastern Venezuela and in the territory of Amapá in northeastern Brazil (Evans and Meggers 1957), the Sipaliwini and Parú savannahs of Suriname (Boomert 1975, 1977; Frikel 1961, 1969) and by Hurault, Frenay and Raoux (1956), who recorded stone alignments in granite outcrops atop the Mitaraka Massif in French Guiana. In the Rupununi, the alignments recorded by Brown (1876), Farabee (1918), Henderson (1952), Roth (1929) and Williams (1979a) include a range of types.

Meggers and Evans (1957) note the similarity of structures occurring in the Aruã Phase of the Territory of Amapá in Brazil to those of Guyana. They presumed that stone alignments were not of Rupununi Phase origin, having been introduced from the Amazon. In contrast, Boomert (1981:144-145) claims that stone alignments could have originated independently from similar socio-religious concepts. Boomert's work describes six categories or types. These include rows of spaced stones, circles of spaced stones, single standing stones known as "menhirs" piles of stones, stone figures, and walls of stone. The Lukobar Mountain alignment consists of a single row of spaced stones and stone figures (Plew and Pereira 2000) (Figure 29).

The single row of stones is comparable to those described by Brown (1876) east of the Ireng River and those reported by Williams (1979a) in the vicinity of Makatau Mountain south of Aishalton. Williams reported linear rows of spaced stones measuring 106 and 75 m in length.

The larger of these consisted of 750 quartz cobbles and the smaller of 122 granite cobbles. The larger alignment situated on a small hillock to the east of Makatau Mountain ends in a short fork enclosed on its third side to form a triangle. The Lukobar alignment (48 m) is smaller than those reported by Williams (1979a) but like the larger of the Makatau alignments is configured into circular and rectangular forms constituting part of the same alignment. The function of the alignments remains speculative though the locations and the material associations would seem to support the ceremonial/ritual function ascribed to them by Evans and Meggers (1960). Roth (1929) reports that the alignments served as a reminder of the numbers of individuals slain in battle, a report reiterated to us by Wapishana informants. Roth (1929) also observed that alignments may have served as "signs or signals on the road." Regardless of function, Rupununi Plain sherds recovered from the Lukobar locality indicate that stone alignments are associated with the Rupununi Phase.

Location	Site	Geometric								Anthropomorphic				Phyto-morphic	Total
		Type i	Type ii	Type iii	Type iv	Type v	Type vi	Type vii	Non-diagnostic	Symmetric	Asymmetric	Non-diagnostic	Naturalistic	Schematic	
Makatau Savanna	S-1	14	18			24									56
	S-2	1				1									2
	S-3	1	1	1	2	13			1	1					20
	S-4					1									1
	S-5		1						1	1					3
	S-6					1				1					2
	S-7	1				1									2
Makatau Mountain	S-8	25	2	3	12	6	2		13	15					78
	S-9	1	1			7									9
Makatau Cave	S-10	3	12			9			12						36
	S-11				10	20	14			27					71
	S-12				15	6			3	31	5				60
	S-13	1			10	10	23			9					53
	S-14					2									2
	S-15					1				13					14
	S-16		9			11			5						25
Makatau Rockshelters	S-17	5	5			11	4	1	2	13					41
	S-18					3				15			1		19
Warau-N	S-19									2					2
Kazarwau-Kyuzu	S-20	1					1	1	4						7
	S-21	1								1					2
Katanairn	S-22	4	11	2	19	35		4	21	14		1	3	4	118
	S-23		3				2		2	1	3				11
	S-24			1	3	1			2	2	9				18
	S-25	2	1												3
	S-26	1				1									2
	S-27	2				1			2						5
Dredon	S-28	2				1			1						4
Waramasi	S-29	1							2						3
Kawarwau-nau	S-30	6	1						5	4				1	17
		72	65	7	71	166	43	8	73	61	93	18	4	5	686

(from Williams 1978)

Table 5. Classification of Motifs of the Aishalton Complex

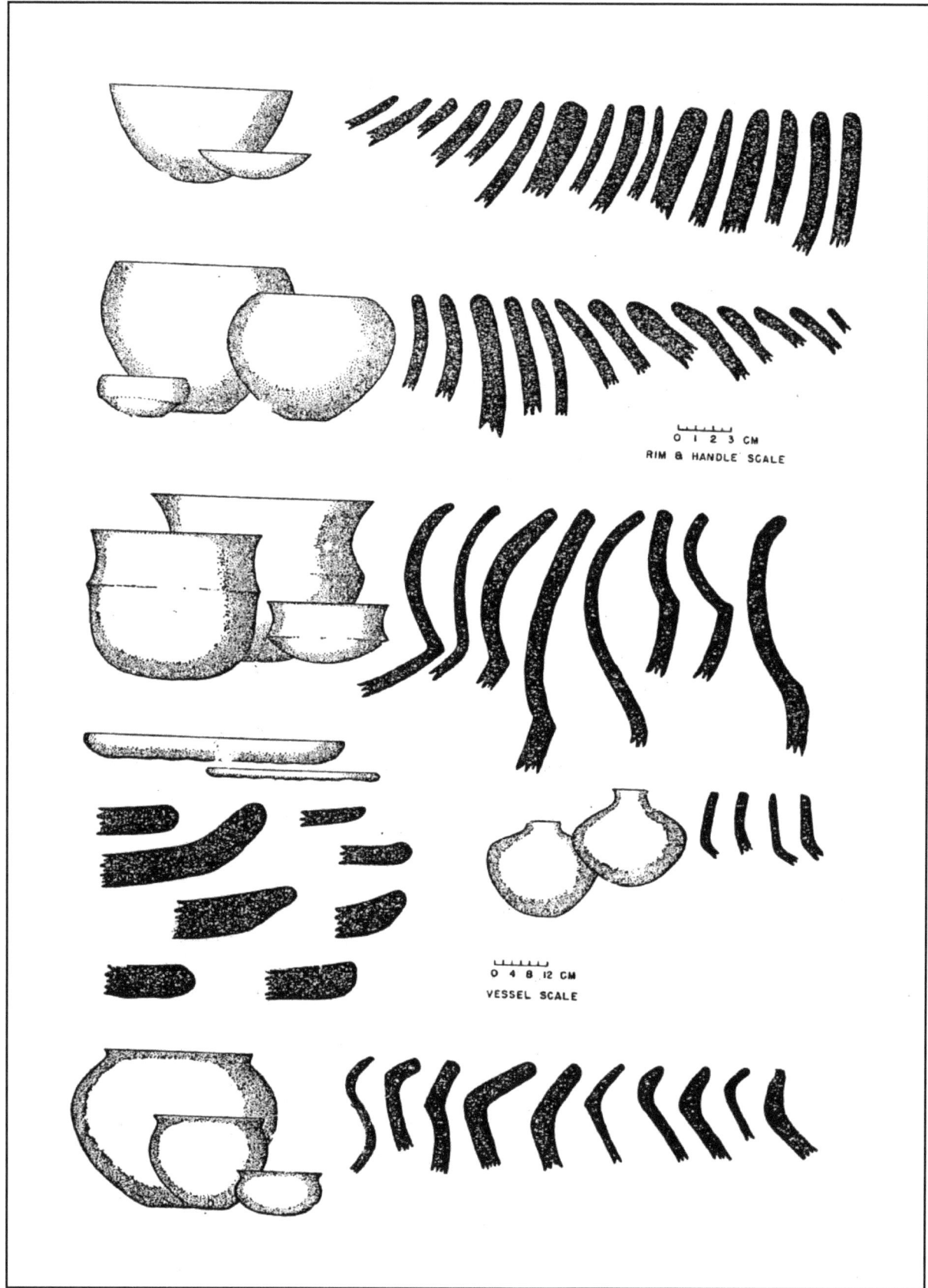

Figure 28. Kanuku and Rupununi Phase Vessel Forms (from Evans and Meggers 1960:308

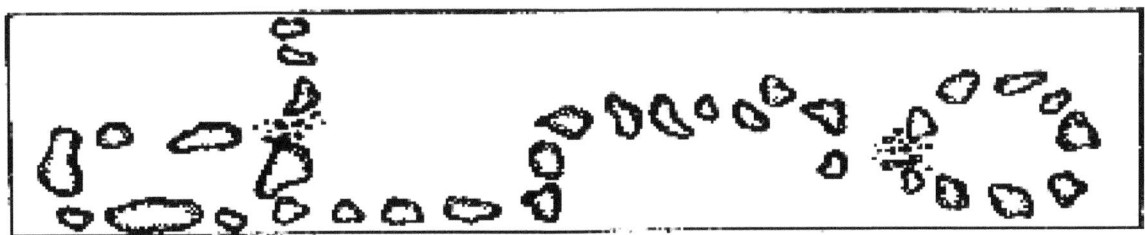

Figure 29. Stone Alignment at Lukobar Mountain

The Archaeology of Shiriri Mountain Cemetery

A cemetery on Shiriri Mountain indicates some greater variation in mortuary practice than that described by Evans and Meggers (1960) who note the use of ledges and walls of granite boulders for placement of burial jars (Figure 30). These are typically few in number, occasionally isolated, and in some instances accompanied by large vessels of the Kanuku Plain type placed in an inverted position relative to burial jars to serve as lids (Figure 31). Though the vessel types reported by Evans and Meggers (1960) are relatively similar to the range of vessels present at the Shiriri Mountain cemetery (IX-2:79), Shiriri appears to represent a funerary context used many times over an extended period. In addition, the face of the rockshelter is covered by red pictographs. These include a geometric configuration of connected rectangles and a series of dot and line patterns. The geometric motif is located just above the stone platform at the base of the shelter where the vessels were placed. Above the rectangles is a series of fine red lines in lateral groupings. To the east, a group of lines and dots was found in variable configurations. Lines are often situated one above another. Four ceramic vessels were recovered from the cemetery. These include four small globular vessels. Surface and core color indicate that three of the vessels belong to the type Rupununi Plain while one is Kanuku Plain. A red vessel having nine orange-red zig-zag lines painted vertically between the lip and carination of the vessel was recovered (see Figure 31).

Vessels have constricted necks but variable sizes. There is no evidence of the use of open vessels as lids. Instead, small ceramic disks measuring 4-6 cm in diameter were fastened or sealed over the mouth by small daubs of yellowish clay measuring approximately 1-1.5 cm in diameter. While Evans and Meggers (1960:295) report that the only cremated remains from the Rupununi Phase were found in a single vessel from Tamiro-Wau cemetery, it appears that all vessels at Shiriri contained cremated remains (Plew and Pereira 2000).

Hence, the Shiriri cemetery is distinct with respect to context, to sealing of vessels and to the common practice of cremation, a form of disposal not practiced by the historic Wapishana (Plew and Pereira 2000). It appears that the remains had been exposed to high temperatures with only distal ends of upper and lower limbs bones present. Several individuals are represented, with one small vessel appearing to contain the remains of an infant.

The Shiriri cemetery is unusual in being associated with pictographic rock art, which not only has not been archaeologically reported in the Rupununi but also consists of motifs not common in petroglyphic panels of Aishalton (Williams 1979a) and of the Essequibo and Kassikaityu Rivers (Williams 1979b and 1985b). The exceptions are Brown's (1876) and Baldwin's (1946) passing references to painted figures.

The Shiriri cemetery pictographs consist of red painted lines and dots that appear to be grouped together and a fairly large panel of connected diamond motifs just above the floor of the shelter. Such diamond motifs are not common in the area. Although Williams (1979a: 22-24) describes two small isolated examples at Makatau Cave to the south, the motif is clearly insignificant in the Aishalton style. The presence of pictographic figures at the Shiriri cemetery implies that red pictographic art may be a facilitating agency of rituals associated with certain burial contexts in late horizons.

Of further significance is the possibility that the orange-red painted vessel from Shiriri reflects additional aspects of Rupununi ritual. Williams (2004) has described a Classic period Mabaruma hands-to-face funerary motif on a figure common throughout portions of Amazonia which is similar to that recovered at Shiriri Mountain. The figurine, which was recovered from a Post Classic cemetery of the Abary phase at Mon Repos on the Demerara coast and in an Apostederan assemblage at Kumuku Hill, is distinctive in the wavy locks motif placed on the back of the neck as a directional device in mortuary ritual (Williams 2004:301). The presence of the motif in the Rupununi suggests the possibility of a rather broad pattern of mortuary symbolism which may have been shared by many peoples over a rather large area and for an extended period of time.

Figure 30. Shiriri Mountain Cemetery with Ceramic Vessels in Foreground

Figure 31. Sealed Vessel, Shiriri Mountain Cemetery

Figure 32. Painted Vessel from Shiriri Mountain

In general, the Shiriri Mountain survey (Plew and Pereira 2001) confirmed earlier observations by Evans and Meggers (1960) and Williams (1979a) regarding the distribution of cultural materials and site types. The survey suggests, however, greater variability in site types as indicated by the discoveries of a lithic workshop station and of the Lukobar Mountain stone alignment, and by the Shiriri Mountain cemetery, which suggests a more elaborate set of ritual and mortuary practices. While recovery of red painted pottery, the description of pictographic rock art, and association of a stone alignment complex with the Rupununi Phase are of specific historical interest, our conclusion is that much additional work is required before a complete understanding of the use of the south savannahs and of the Rupununi Phase is possible.

Although previous archaeological investigations demonstrate the wealth and variability of archeological resources within the region of the south Savannahs, it remains unclear whether the patterns described by Evans and Meggers (1960), Williams (1979a) and Plew and Pereira (2001, 2002) are consistent throughout the area or whether a greater variability in lifeways of hunter-gatherers is to be found, as has been suggested by Williams (1985b).

Recent Archaeological Survey in the Vicinity of the Kanuku Mountains

Archaeological reconnaissance of areas along the western flank of the Kanuku Mountains in the vicinity of Moco-Moco village and the Sawariwau River near Imprenza recorded several archaeological sites (Plew, Mercer and Sundell 2001). These include a lithic workshop/manufacturing station, pollisoirs, burial localities and a probable 19th century village site containing Rupununi Plain pottery. Most notable are two pollisoir locations, a cairn burial and a probable 19th century village site.

Four types of pollisoir were noted at two sites along the Sawariwau River near Imprenza (Figure 33). Type 1 polliosoirs include shallow circular to oval basins measuring 15-30 cm in diameter, while Type 2 are elongated features having widths of 8-9 cm and lengths between 18 and 20 cm. Type 3 consist of narrow elongates measuring ca. 20 cm in length, 3-4 cm in width and 2 cm in depth. Type 4 pollisoirs are large shallow trough-like features set end-to-end and measuring 20 by 30 cm. Over sixty individual features were noted (see Table 6). Pollisoirs have not been routinely described in the Rupununi, making the Sawariwau finds relatively unique. The presence of pollisoir at differing depth levels of the river suggests a pattern similar to that described by

	Type 1	Type 2	Type 3	Type 4
Site 14-1:84	20	6	3	1
Site 14-1:85	10	4	0	1

Table 6. Groundstone Features Near Imprenza

Williams (1979a) in which fish petrogylphs were positioned to coincide with variable water levels (Plew, Mercer and Sundell 2001).

East of the village of Moco-Moco is located an apparent abandoned village site covering an area of 100 x 60 m. Though no evidence of house floors or remnants were observed, fragments of wattle and daub and brick were noted. Two archaeological features were documented consisting of an apparent hearth and refuse dump and a possible stone-lined cooking feature that includes the remains of a pottery vessel. The site contains historic bottle glass, metal fragments, and both plain and decorated porcelain of types similar to those described by Evans and Meggers (1960) and considered to date to the early 19th century. Most notably, twenty sherds of the type Rupununi Plain were recovered at the location. This tends to support Evans and Meggers' (1960) assertion that the Rupununi Phase extended into the historic period.

In addition to recording a significant number of pollisoirs and an important 19th century village site, the survey identified a burial locality unlike those previously described by Evans and Meggers (1960) and by Plew and Pereira in 2000. North of the Moco-Moco trail are two large boulder shelters. Along the south edge of the more northerly situated boulder is a cairn burial. The burial contains the remains of a robust male placed on a stone slab measuring approximately one meter by 70 cm and covered by stones to an approximate height of some 70 centimeters. Quantities of Kanuku Plain pottery sherds are scattered about the burial area and the slope of the rockshelter (Figure 34).

The findings of the west Kanuku survey reaffirm what is presently known of the prehistory of the Rupununi, suggesting that the pattern is considerably more varied than previously known. While the discovery of new site types will allow assessment of the greater variability of the Rupununi Phase, identification, evaluation, and dating of additional habitation sites will permit a more compete understanding of the Rupununi Phase peoples in the early historic period.

Archaeological Sites Near Shulinab and Mariwau: Further Evidence of Rupununi Funerary Practices

Archaeological survey has also identified archaeological sites in the vicinity of Shulinab and Mariwau Villages some forty miles south of Lethem (Figure 35). In the mountains east of Shulinab Village, the survey located a rock alignment complex consisting of stacked stones, cairns, and a rectangular feature resembling the range of features described by Evans and Meggers (1959) in the Amapá region of Brazil and the Parú savannahs of Suriname (Boomert 1975, 1977). The alignment, however, most closely resembles that described by Williams (1979) at Makatau Mountain and by Plew and Pereira (2000) at Lukobar Mountain near Shiriri.

The Skull Mountain cemetery is located in a rockshelter below the rock alignment/"war-bench" described above. The shelter rises some 20 m above its floor and measures approximately 35 x 8 x 12 m. Situated near the center of the rockshelter are nineteen ceramic vessels. The largest, measuring 70 cm in diameter, contains the remains of three male individuals appearing to have been in their twenties at the time of death. A single female mandible was situated under ceramic sherds near the back of the shelter. While the vessels vary greatly in size, all but two are Kanuku Plain (Plew and Saras 2002, Table 7). The remaining large vessels are of the type Rupununi Plain. All are round-bottomed, and none appear to have been sealed, similar to the vessels associated with the cairn burial near Moco-Moco Creek. While the majority were open-mouthed, a few of the smaller ones possessed incurved necks. This is of note since many of the vessels at Shiriri were sealed with clay lids, though all were constricted-necked vessels. Of equal interest is the presence of pictographic rock art in the form of parallel smudges, lines, dissected circles, a U-shaped configuration and opposed rectangles (Plew and Pereira 2001). The nature of the smudges may reflect a phosgene-enhanced state of its producers (see Williams 2004:180-181 for discussion).

An additionally important discovery was made in mountains near Mariwau Village where burial urns were recessed into pits excavated into an open saddle some 200 m above the savannah floor (Figure 36). Though two of the features had been looted, the third remained intact. Two Kanuku Plain vessels were superimposed and stabilized by stones placed around the base of the upper vessel. To date, this is the first recording of this type of burial in the Rupununi.

Figure 33. Groundstone Features near Imprenza

Figure 34. Cairn Burial Near Moco-Moco

Figure 35. Burial Vessels at Rockshelter Near Shulinab Village

The Archaeology of the Rupununi Savannah

Number	Height	Diameter	Mouth	Type
1		26		Kanuku Plain
2		26		Kanuku Plain
3		34		Kanuku Plain
4	48	38		Kanuku Plain
5	38	30	18	Kanuku Plain
6	35	30	16	Kanuku Plain
7	35	16		Kanuku Plain
8	37	30		Kanuku Plain
9	32	30		Kanuku Plain
10	25	22	8	Kanuku Plain
11	48	38	42	Rupununi Plain
12	29	20		Kanuku Plain
13	33	32		Kanuku Plain
14	53	70	39	Rupununi Plain
15		30		Kanuku Plain
16		32		Kanuku Plain
17		24		Kanuku Plain
18	6	10	8	Kanuku Plain
19	6	9		Kanuku Plain

*Most vessels were broken. Measurements were based on greatest and most complete dimensions.

*Table 7. Ceramic Vessels from Site IX-2-91**

Figure 36. Burial Vessels from Site Near Mariwau

The Archaeology of Toka and Yupukari

Recent work in the vicinity of Yupukari and Toka villages in the north Rupununi has also cast light on the general occupations of the area (Plew and Pereira 2002). In and around Toka, pollisoirs similar to those at Imprenza on the Sauriwau River were noted, as was a mountaintop village with cooking areas and a range of decorated and painted ceramics (Figure 37). In addition, a new type of cemetery characterized by earthen and stone mounds was recorded, as were petroglyphs of the Enumerative style on Banuni Creek south of Toka (Plew and Pereira 2002).

The investigations reported here suggest a generally greater variability in site types than previously known (cf. Evans and Meggers 1960; Plew and Pereira 2001; Plew, Mercer and Sundell 2001). First, the results suggest that open ceramic scatters/sites may b expected to occur in locations other than adjacent to major water sources, as is the case with the recently recorded mountaintop village near Toka. Secondly, there appears to be a common pattern of stone alignment construction in site areas locally known as "war-benches," and thirdly, pictographic rock art is associated with some burial localities but not all. The findings further suggest that burials are not gender specific, are sometimes situated in open areas, and again are quite varied, as is demonstrated by the superimposition of burial urns at some sites. Though Evans and Meggers (1960) described vessels recessed into rockshelter floors, the discoveries at Mariwau appear to be the first instance reported in which vessels were placed in an open area.

Recent investigations within the North Rupununi allow for the assessment of whether significant differences of settlement exist between the north and south savannahs. Such an assessment should provide insights regarding the methods and seasonality of resource use and the potential optimality of different resources and strategies, as well as the relative importance of hunting and gathering to horticulture in regard to the seasonal versus the annual importance of fishing to hunting and horticulture. In addition, examining the relationships between the areas should allow for a better understanding of tool stone acquisition and distribution as well as of the manufacture of lithic and ceramic items and their distribution. This will overall enhance our knowledge of the ritual and religious sites in the region.

Summary

The archaeology of the Rupununi Savannahs documents possible early Paleo-Indians and more extensive Archaic and Horticultural occupations. A Paleo-Indian presence is indicated by paleo-type points found near the Ireng River and in the vicinity of Mariwau in the south savannahs. Though present evidence is extremely limited, the nature of the Pleistocene environment logically suggests the likelihood of further delineation of the pattern. Notably, and in contrast with Williams' (1985a) assertions that early Paleo-Indians were big game hunters, it seems likely that evidence may be found in support of a pattern of Paleo-Indian foraging in the future. The Archaic pattern is assumed to date as early as 5,000 B.CA. and is characterized by a range of chipped and portable groundstone artifacts as well as permanent features that include grinding surface/depressions and sharpening grooves (*pollisoirs*). In addition, geometric rock alignments, stone piles (cairns), and circles are common. Further important is the widespread manufacture of petroglyphic rock art. The rock art of Aishalton and Makatau Mountain include 30 petroglyph sites comprised of 686 motifs carved on granite boulders. Elements consisting mainly of bimorphic and geometric motifs were inscribed using a broad line and deep groove technique that often combines dots and furrows with bimorphic and geometric motifs. Williams (1979a, 1985a) argues that varied combinations of motifs signed the presence of resources in different areas. This association is thought to have linked rituals related to subsistence, though it is unclear whether the local shamans or *peaiman*s produced the rock art. Williams (1979a), based on excavations along the margins of the granite boulders, reports the recovery of stone tools he believes to have been associated with the manufacture of the rock art.

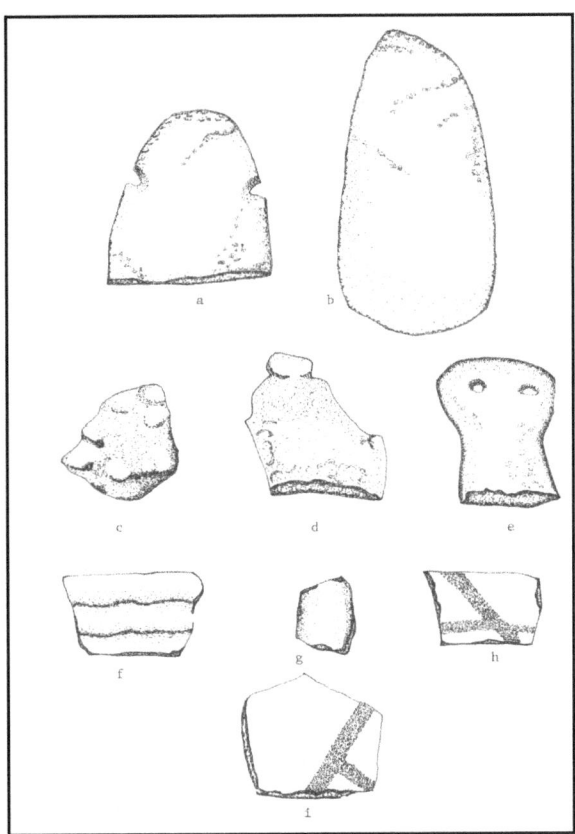

Figure 37. Artifacts from Toka Village: a-b, Stone Axes; c-e, Adornos; f, Unfinished Coiled sherd; g, Incised Sherd; h, Black-on-White Sherd; i, Red-on-Orange Sherd

The Horticultural Period is associated with pottery of the Rupununi Phase. Several Rupununi phase sites contain 18th and 19th century European trade goods. Two pottery types, Rupununi Plain and Kanuku Plain, constitute the majority of the ceramic inventory. Forms include deep bowls with steep walls, globular bowls and jars with rounded walls and incurving and rounded lips and carinated vessels forming round to sloping shoulders. Surface color ranges typically from orange to reddish orange to reddish brown. A few unnamed sherds include decoration in the form of appliqué, punctuates, white paint and white and red slips. Other ceramic artifacts include pottery rests, disks and anthropomorphic figurines. Chipped and groundstone artifacts include anvils, choppers, grooved axes, hoes, manos, metates, hammerstones, and stone bowl fragments. The settlement pattern includes habitation sites (open villages), manufacturing stations, fishing sites, ceremonial sites (rock alignments), cemetery sites, and rock art locations (see Plew n.d.). Recent investigations suggest a broad range of activities and site types within the area as evidenced by the elaborate cemeteries at Shiriri Mountain and near Mariwau and in the variation within specific site types as with groundstone features near the Sawariwau River. The diversity of Rupununi settlement reflects a varied savannah environment in which Amerindians utilized open terrain along streams and rivers for habitation, adjacent bush islands for farming or gardening, and higher elevations within the mountains for ritual practice and for cemeteries.

Type	Number
Habitation	30
Cemetery	16
Petroglyphs	3
Pictographs	2
Lithic Workshop	2
Groundstone Features	2
Rock Alignments	5

Table 8. Distribution of Rupununi Phase Sites by Type

XI. The Central Guyana Rainforest: Archaeology in Iwokrama

The archaeology of Iwokrama provides important data for interpreting not only forest adaptations in Guyana and the surrounding areas but also the simultaneous use of the forest and savannah as part of a broader settlement regime (Figure 38). The overview of Iwokrama archaeology is based upon surveys and test excavations conducted by Williams (1996) and later by Plew (2002, 2003, n.d.).

Williams (1996) participated in two short exploratory surveys in May 1993 that served as the basis for his more formal survey of the Iwokrama conducted in March 1994. Relying upon work by Meggers and Evans (1960) in the Pakaraimas and his own work on the Mazaruni, Potaro, and Essequibo Rivers (Williams n.d., a-c), he sought to predict the nature of archaeological sites and occupations within the reserve. His explorations followed an intuitive strategy in which effort was maximized by conducting a linear survey along stream and river courses. He (1996) analyzed the data within a cultural-historical framework of the Paleo-Indian, Archaic, Horticultural, and Historic Periods. He also sought to evaluate the nature of the so-called "refuge theory" positing Holocene Period climatic fluctuations that reflect expanding and coalescing conditions of wetness and aridity. In particular, Williams (1978) contends that archaeological evidence from Seba on the coast and Quartz Island (n.d.d) in the rain forest near the Mazaruni River documents these fluctuations. In addition, he argues for (1979b, 1985a) a fisheries management strategy which served to identify the use of differing technologies and species at different seasons and locations along rivers and streams within the reserve.

He (1996) also argued for a relationship between forest peoples and those utilizing the savannah as part of a broader regional settlement. More recently, Plew (2002, 2003) has conducted surveys and test excavations in the Iwokrama Mountains and along the Essequibo River near the field station that expanded the settlement variation posited by Williams (1996) (Figure 39).

The Paleo-Indian Period

The Paleo-Indian Period, which dates between 11,500 and 7,000 years ago, is not presently documented within the reserve. Neither Williams (1996) nor Plew (2002) identifies materials or sites dating to the period. If, as Williams (1985) suggests, the economic pursuits of Paleo-Indians are associated with a "Big-Game" orientation characteristic of more open parklands/savannah country, evidence within the reserve may be limited. If there occurred extended periods of drought during late Pleistocene or Early Holocene, evidence may exist in some locations. The absence of data may also reflect the level of archaeological samplingwithin the reserve and in Guyana generally.

In Guyana, Williams (1985b) reports on a Paleo-like point from the Ireng River. Additionally, Plew (1997) has identified three triangular quartz specimens in the Im Thurn collections at Cambridge University as collected near the Barima River, a second on the Ireng and a third from the Essequibo. An additional specimen from the Mariwau area in the Rupununi has been identified (Plew and Saras 2001).

The Archaic Period

The Archaic Period, dating between 7,000 and 3,500 years ago, is characterized by a pattern of broad spectrum foraging associated with a wide range of sites including artificial groundstone depressions, chipping stations/manufacturing locations, petroglyphs and isolated artifacts. Because the Archaic economic strategy reflects considerable use of the forest, a range of new "groundstone" tools including axes, adzes, and other woodworking and plant processing tools appears in the archaeological record here for the first time. Some items are associated with the manufacture and use of artificial depressions consisting of open basins used for plant processing and for sharpening grooves.

Petroglyphs include stylistic elements characteristic of the so-called Enumerative and Fish-Trap styles, which Williams (1985a) believed to be associated with different time periods, cultural traditions, and subsistence strategies. Absent from the area are design motifs characteristic of the Timehri pictographic style. The enumerative style, while considered the oldest, includes geometric, anthropomorphic, and zoomorphic elements while the Fish-Trap style glyphs were "sign-posted" on rocks identifying different species and seasonal locations. The latter style is thought by Williams (1985a) to be associated with periods of reduced precipitation during the late Holocene. Most notable is his report (1996) of the first occurrence of the so-called Cuneiform glyph in Guyana. The glyph is a sub-variant of the Enumerative style and is found mainly on the Siparuni River. Specifically, it is an inscription technique in which a narrow "v"-shaped groove is cut into the stone in the manufacture of the glyph. As such it represents more the method of manufacture than a petroglyphic style. Enumerative style, which is most commonly represented in the rock art of Iwokrama, is found on the Essequibo as far as Waraputa Falls and on the Buro-Buro to Dakali Falls. The Fish-Trap style is known from the "spring-basket trap" glyph at Kurukupari on the Essequibo. Glyphs of the Fish-Trap style are thought to be associated with different water levels, as suggested by those at Inscription Rock on the Buro-Buro River. At Sharples, Williams reports a unique and as yet unreported style described as including an "integrated lozenge."

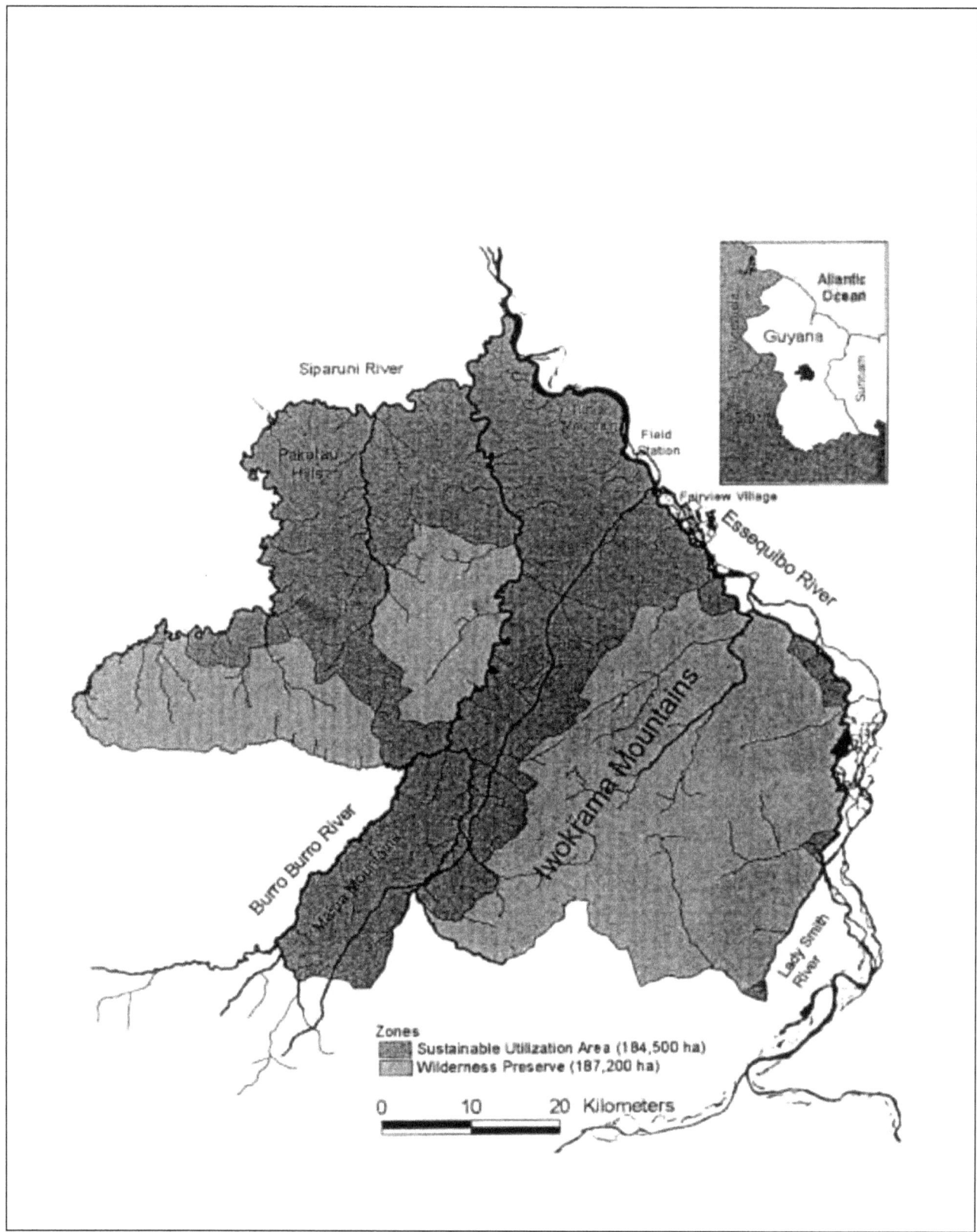

Figure 38. General Location of the Iwokrama Reserve

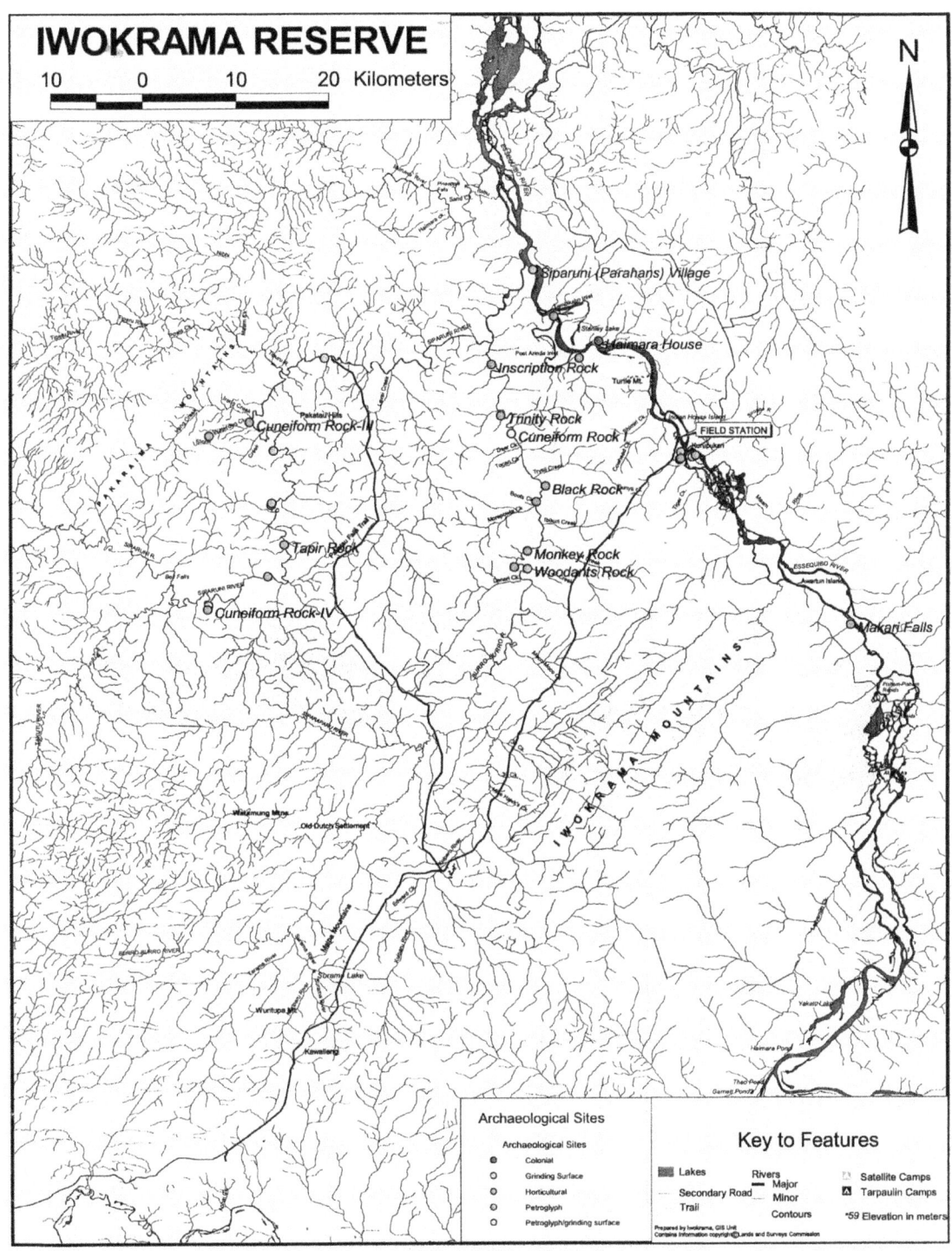

Figure 39. Map Showing the Location of Archaeological Sites within Iwokrama

While it appears that rock art of the Enumerative, Cuneiform, and Fish-Trap styles reflects varying functions, it is unclear as to whether the styles represent different cultural traditions (ethnic populations) and/or different time periods, since most rock art is undatable. Further, while Williams' (1985a) hypothesis regarding fisheries management has great interpretive value, it does not appear possible on the basis of present evidence to

Sites	Drainage	Type/Style
Kurupukari Landing	Essequibo	Enumerative
Kurupukari Falls	Essequibo	Enumerative/Fishtrap
Sharples Island	Essequibo	Fishtrap/Enumerative
Turtle Pond	Essequibo	Fishtrap
Cuneiform Rock-4	Essequibo	Cuneiform
Cuneiform Rock-1	Siparuni	Cuneiform
Cuneiform Rock-2	Siparuni	Cuneiform
Cuneiform Rock-3	Siparuni	Cuneiform
Black Rock	Burro Burro	Enumerative
Duckla Falls	Burro Burro	Enumerative
Monkey Falls	Burro Burro	Undetermined
Woodants Rock	Burro Burro	Fishtrap
Inscription Rock	Burro Burro	Enumerative
Horseshoe Island	Burro Burro	Fishtrap
Unnamed Creek	Burro Burro	Undetermined
Iwokrama Mountain	Burro Burro	Enumerative
Mile Thirty-Eight Creek	Burro Burro	Undetermined
First Rock	Takutu	Enumerative
Second Rock	Takutu	Cuneiform
Third Rock	Takutu	Cuneiform

Table 9. Iwokrama Petroglyph Sites

Groundstone Features (Artificial Depressions and Sharpening Grooves)

One of the most notable categories of archaeological sites within the Iwokrama forest is the groundstone features that occur in numerous locations along the major rivers. The features include shallow basin depressions used for processing plants and steeply incised grooves believed to be used for sharpening axes, adzes, and other woodworking implements. The features Williams (1985b) has commonly referred to as "pollisoirs" have not been typed and recorded in many areas. They occur in a variety of forms and often with the shallow basin depressions.

Williams (1996) reported groundstone features on the Siparuni, Buro-Buro, and the Essequibo Rivers. The most diverse and extensive of these occur on the Siparuni, where six individual sites contain a total of 926 groundstone features, including both open dish-like depressions and "sharpening" grooves. Though some have been noted at Electric Eel Rock (N=34), Tapir Rock (N=34), Trinity Rock (N=3), and Pakatau Falls (N=3), 92% occur at Big "S" Falls. Williams (1996) notes a rather equal distribution on the left (N=414) and right (N=434) river banks and observes that sharpening grooves, which are not common, also exhibit a relatively equal distribution between river banks. On the Buro-Buro River, 37 depressions were noted with 68% (n=24) located at Monkey Falls. Very few sharpening grooves were observed. The number of reported depressions on the Essequibo River also varied greatly. A total of 25 were noted at Kurukupari Falls, while 33 were observed at Sharples. The largest number occurred at Cuneiform Rock, where 136 were noted. In general, few sharpening grooves were noted (see Table 10).

Williams (1996) does not develop a formal typology of groundstone features though he describes three types that include circular to ovoid depressions, ellipsoids resulting from longitudinal grinding of preforms into specific tools/implements, and ellipsoids from sharpening the edges of cutting tools. He assumes that size grades in the latter reflect the use of different grooves to sharpen different types of tools. Plew, Mercer, and Sundell (2001) have developed a typology of four groundstone features based on findings on the Sauriwau River in the Rupununi which seem applicable to the variability in features within Iwokrama. The typology recognizes form, size, and spatial alignment. Type 1 features consist of shallow (1-2 cm) circular-to-oval basins measuring between 15-30 cm in diameter. Type 2 features are elongated depressions having widths between 8 and 9 cm, lengths from 18 to 20 cm, and average depths of 4 cm. Type 3 features are narrow and average 20 cm in length, 3-4 cm in width and 2 cm in depth. Type 3 features often occur in rows, while Type 4 features include large shallow trough-basin features set end-to-end in rows. The majority of the features recorded by Williams (1996) appear to fall within the range of Type 1, with few sharpening grooves reported fitting Type 2 features (Tables 10 and 11).

Lithic Chipping/Manufacturing Station

Williams (1996) reports thousands of lithic flakes and artifacts on the left bank of the Buro-Buro River at Inscription Rock, an area of extensive quartz outcroppings. These include two bifacially worked axes (12 x 6 x 3 cm and 9.5 x 10 x 3.5 cm) and two large plano-convex choppers notable since very few lithic quarries and/or workshops have been recorded within the area.

River	Sites	Basin Depressions	Sharpening Grooves
Essequibo			
	Reserve Base Camp	4	-
	Cuneiform Rock	136	-
Siparuni			
	Cuneiform Rock	2	-
	Electric Eel	18	13
	Tapir Rock	33	1
	Little "S" Falls	12	-
	Big "S" Falls	853	129
	Trinity Rock	3	-
	Pakatan	3	-
Burro Burro			
	Monkey Falls	24	-
	Black Rock	22	2
	Unnamed Rock	8	1
	Dukali Falls	3	-

(after Williams n.d.)

Table 10. Distribution Of Basin Depressions And Sharpening Grooves By Drainage And Site

Length cm	Depth				
	0-10 mm	11-20 mm	21-30 mm	31-40 mm	41-50 mm
0-10 cm	2	-	-	-	-
11-20 cm	4	5	-	-	-
21-30 cm	24	21	11	5	-
31-40 cm	7	18	8	3	1
41-50 cm	-	3	3	3	-

(after Williams n.d.)

Table 11. Big "S" Falls (V111 – 2:39)lationships Of Length To Depth In 118 Sharpening Grooves

Archaic Sites in the Iwokrama Mountains

An archaeological survey of the eastern flank of the Iwokrama Mountains has identified an Archaic occupation/use of areas beyond the major rivers (Plew 2002). This suggests that the Archaic settlement pattern is one in which prehistoric peoples visited and used areas/resources throughout the region and which contrasts with the pattern suggested by Williams' (1996) surveys.

The survey strategy involved gradual ascent of the mountain from a base camp established some two miles east of the Georgetown-Lethem road along an unnamed stream course, with descent along its western face. The survey inspected landscape features considered likely archaeological sites, including streams, seeps, boulders along streams, rock outcrops, stone piles, and large rock boulders near summits.

The survey identified two petroglyph sites on secondary and tertiary stream courses. The petroglyphic elements resemble in general the Enumerative Petroglyph Tradition elements reported elsewhere in the reserve (Plew 2003). The first site is located approximately two kilometers east of the trailhead on a small intermittent stream measuring no more than three meters across and characterized by numerous granite boulders. Like most of the area, the granite is covered by a dark magnesium oxide. Two generally bi-centric circles on a west-facing boulder measure roughly one meter in diameter. The elements measure 40 x 29 cm and 23 x 20 x 39 cm. The style is a broad-line deep gravure motif. The gravures are approximately 3 cm wide and 1-2 cm in depth. The second set of elements was noted along a 15 m wide stream approximately one kilometer east of the first locality and 200 m north of the base camp. The elements consist of straight lines, curvilinear elements and a completely pecked, heart-shaped element. One single element appears to represent a serpent. The elements are situated on flat boulders along the stream course and occur over an area of approximately 3 m in what are essentially two panels. The larger of these covers an area of about 50 x 30 cm. A single curvilinear motif measures 25 x 36 cm. The gravures are roughly 2-3 cm in width and 1-2 cm in depth. In the one instance, the edges of the boulders forming angles have been pecked to smooth surfaces. All motifs appeared above the present water line.

The findings of the recent survey are significant because they indicate the presence of human groups in areas beyond the major rivers. In this regard, the discovery of petroglyphs on secondary and tertiary streams/drainages indicates that prehistoric Amerindians who are known to have inhabited and utilized the major river courses also made use of areas in the interior forest and that these areas were not exclusively associated with subsistence activities. Of further significance is the identification of numerous locations on the mountain that could have served as short-term habitation sites and as cemetery or burial localities. The area inspected, though small relative to the total area of the Iwokrama Mountains, was characterized by rock outcrops and boulder shelters that are known to have been utilized by Amerindians. Team informants reported areas within the Iwokrama very similar to locations around the area of Toka to the south where recent discoveries of the pattern have been made (Plew and Pereira 2002). Also notable is the discovery of rock art in settings above present water levels. This raises questions regarding Williams' (1996) view that desiccation of the forest occurred periodically during the Holocene.

Horticultural Period

During the Horticultural Period dating between 3,500 B.P. and the Historic period, occupation in Iwokrama is documented by the recording of seven archaeological sites containing evidence of pottery. Sites dating into the Horticultural Period have been found on the Essequibo

Figure 40. Tertiary Stream, East Face, Iwokrama Mountains

(N=7) and the Siparuni (N=1). Test excavations have been conducted by Plew (2002) at four locations on the Essequibo, near Kurukupari Falls at Errol's Landing, and on Alexis Marcel's Island, as well as at Makari Falls (Williams 1996) and at the Reserve Base Camp (Field Station) and a Big "S" Falls on the Siparuni (Williams 1996; Plew n.d.).

Essequibo River

Important to defining horticultural occupations in the reserve are excavations conducted by Williams (1996) at Errol's Landing. Just above Kurukupari Falls on a river terrace some 3 m above low water levels, Williams (1996) excavated a 2 x 2 m test unit to a depth of 80 cm. The 0-15 cm level consisted of *terre preta* soil containing rootlets, charcoal, potsherds (N=314), and lithic detritus. Level 15-30 cm was similar to the 0-15 level with the exception of an increase in the numbers of pebbles and a decrease in charcoal. Pottery sherds totaled 802 were found throughout the level. Level 30-45 saw an increase in the density of pebbles but a decrease in the number of potsherds (N=390). An area of intense burning yielded a charcoal sample.

Level 45-60 saw no change in soil type but an increase in pebble size and density. The density was such that the excavation area was reduced to 1 x 2 m. The sherd count was 112. Level 60-80 was excavated within a 1 x 1 m unit to accommodate the difficulty of excavating through large cobbles. Only nine sherds were recovered, and the excavation was curtailed at 80 cm due to the presence of large rocks. While this site produced the most significant ceramic inventory from the reserve as well as a stone tool assemblage that included a whetstone measuring 6.5 cm in diameter, a hammerstone measuring ca. 7 cm in diameter, a scraper/knife made from a lithic flake measuring between 6-8 cm, a chopper measuring ca. 8 cm in diameter, and a projectile point manufactured from a flake measuring approximately 7 cm in length. Radiocarbon dates of 2080 +/- 70 B.P. (Beta-76246) for the 45-60 cm level and of 2910 +/- 80 B.P. (Beta-76247) were obtained from the lower levels of the site which date into the early Horticultural Period (see Table 5).

The Ceramic Inventory

The ceramic inventory consisted of 1627 sherds of which only 99 (7%) were decorated (Williams 1996). Pottery was manufactured using a coiling technique and temper that consisted of quartz sand, decomposed granite, and caraipé. Unoxidized and oxidized sherds were found with colors ranging from gray-black through ash to tan to brick-orange. Tempering agents appeared to be associated with varying degrees of oxidation with most granite-tempered specimens fully oxidized. Core color varies, with pottery being relatively hard (3.0 Moh), well smoothed, and occasionally burnished (Williams 1996). Painted pottery generally consisted of red-on-white. Incision was reported stained with red pigment. Undecorated vessel forms include seven types. These include open bowls with direct rims and tapered, rounded, beveled, or thickened lips having mouth diameters of 16-40 cm and wall thicknesses of 5.5-8 mm; deep bowls with vertical, incurving or outsloping sidewalls, direct rims with tapered, rounded or beveled lips with mouth diameters of 12-40 cm and wall thicknesses of 4-9 mm; open bowls with flanged rims and

Figure 41. Kurukupari Falls. Rock Art Covered Boulders in Foreground

mouth diameters 24-30 cm; carinated bowls with direct rims and tapered, beveled or interiorly thickened lips and flat bases with mouth diameters 12-30 cm and wall thicknesses 2.5-7.5 mm; a globular jar with constricted mouths with direct rims with tapered rounded or interiorly thickened lip with mouth diameter of 32 cm and vessel wall thickness 6-8 mm; a globular bottle with outsloping or weakly concave-collared neck and direct rim with rounded or tapered lip having a mouth diameter of 6 cm and a wall thickness 6.5 mm; and a griddle with interiorly thickened rim measuring 22 mm and a wall thickness of 17 mm. In general, plain vessel forms resemble those of the Taruma Phase (Evans and Meggers 1960).

Decorated ceramics from Errol's Landing include a range of vessel forms and decoration techniques that include painting, modeling, incising, brushing, scraping, stamping, and fingertip impressions. Ten vessel shapes described by Williams (1996) include open bowls with direct rims painted red-on-white or incised on exterior surfaces; open bowls with a wide range of flanged rims in excess of 20 mm with incised motifs which include broad line "U"-section incisions parallel to the rim and accented by spiral, circular and semi-circular motifs; open bowls with thickened rims measuring between 6-17 mm with interior and exterior incisions; bowls with incurvate walls, flat bases and zoomorphic lugs; flat-based small-mouthed (up to 12 cm) pans with everted lobed rims decorated with a red wash and paired incisions including vertical semicircles bounded by incised horizontals; deep bowls/jars with vertical vessel walls and thickened rims having mouth diameters between 22-36 cm and wall thicknesses between 7-8 mm with "U"-sectioned incisions placed on rim surfaces by fingertip impression; deep bowls with curving to angular shoulders with everted rims and straight vessel walls with "U" sectioned incisions and paired semicircles which are common as are bottles or jars with collared necks and flattened bases having mouth diameters of 6-12 cm, strap handles, and punctated nubbins over a white slip applied to both interior and exterior surfaces and wall thicknesses averaging 6.5 mm; globular jars with walls incurving to constricted mouths measuring 12-30 cm and having vessel wall thicknesses of between 9.5 and 5 mm with roller-stamped lattice of lozenge-shaped units; carinated bowls with direct rims and rounded lips and flanges decorated with "U"-sectioned concentric and three serially arranged vertical semicircles; carinated bowl with incurving upper walls, direct rim, and rounded lip having a mouth diameter of 16 cm and wall thickness of 5 mm with "U"-shaped incisions on upper portion of vessel and paired semicircles bounded by horizontals top and bottom; and thin and punctuated surface decorated with flanged rim and mouth diameter of 40 cm The lid is a thin jar lid decorated with surface punctuations. In general, types resemble those described by Evans and Meggers (1960).

Located immediately east of Sharples Island near Kurukupari Falls, the area around the Alexis Marcel's boat landing produced 65 pottery sherds (Williams 1996). Excavation of a 2 x 2 m test unit using 20 cm arbitrary excavation levels produced an assemblage of both ceramics and stone tools. The upper two levels consisted of white sand containing charcoal and interspersed with historic materials in the uppermost horizons. The 40-60 cm level consisted of white sand that rapidly stained bright orange, contained more clay and was increasingly more compact. No cultural material was found in the level. The unit floor was probed to a level of 80 cm below datum and produced no cultural materials (Williams 1996).

The material culture included stone tools and debris and pottery (Williams 1996). One chipped and one groundstone axe were recovered as were lithic flakes of jasper, which occurs in the Pakaraimas. Undecorated vessels included open bowls with direct rims and tapered, rounded and thickened lips; deep bowls with vertical incurvate walls and direct rims with tapered, rounded or beveled lips; and carinated bowls with excurvate upper walls and direct rims with tapered, beveled or thickened lips. Vessels generally resemble those at Errol's Landing though none possesses a red wash. Decorated ceramics include a globular jar with incurvate walls, constricted mouth, and direct rim with rounded lip. Decoration includes the remnants of a red wash or slip and the latticework of lozenge-shaped units set above the shoulder of the vessel. The latter measures 10-20 mm in maximum diameter (Williams 1996). Williams (1996) does not provide level totals for sherds recovered though it appears that the assemblage was not large.

Williams' (1996) visit to the field station resulted in the collection of 30 sherds from a relatively restricted area south of the administrative/kitchen area and roughly 300 m south of the Essequibo River. Plain sherds in the collection are from carinated bowls with incurvate upper walls, direct rims and tapered, beveled, or thickened lips (N=28). Temper consists of crushed decayed granite. The decorated sherds include one well smoothed, red painted sherd and a second with "U"-shaped incisions 8 mm wide that circle the rim.

Two 1 x 1 m test units were excavated approximately three meters west of the field station boat dock. The units were aligned to magnetic north and excavated in 10 cm levels to an approximate depth of 25 cm. The units were subsequently probed to a depth of ca. 40 cm with no noticeable change in the nature of the deposit or densities of cultural material. The deposit consisted of white sand containing rootlets, and some charcoal and historic artifacts including wood, nails, glass, and metal fragments. Unit 3-4W/0-1N contained at the 10 cm level two plain sherds resembling the type Rupununi Plain. More recent investigation of the area recorded three plain beige-orange sherds (Plew 2002). These measured ca. 7 cm in length and approximately 4 cm in width and were smoothed and resembled the type Rupununi Plain.

Located approximately 3.5 m above water level on a small mound directly back of the riverbank at Makari Falls is a small area of *terre preta* investigated by Williams (1996) during his survey of the Iwokrama reserve. A 2 x 2 m test pit excavated to a depth of 20 cm revealed an almost continuous bed of charcoal but no cultural materials. While Williams (1996) suggests that the site may have been a prehistoric fishing camp, it is unclear whether it dates within the Horticultural Period since a single radiocarbon date was assessed at 90 +/- 50 B.P. (Beta-76249; see Table 12).

From an area located approximately 30 m above Kurukupari on the left band of the Essequibo, Williams (1996) collected 24 sherds eroding from the plaza of a multi-household compound. The sample contained 15 cariapé-tempered and nine sand-tempered sherds that resemble plain types of the Koriabo and Rupununi Phases.

On the right bank of the Essequibo opposite Kurukupari Landing, local excavations recovered two small petaloid axes, a fragment of a large Dutch jar, and two sand and cariapé sherds of an undescribed type (Williams 1996).

Sherds from a large globular jar with collared neck and exteriorly thickened rim from a single ceramic vessel were recovered in a crevice within the Kurupukari Falls (Williams 1996). The mouth of the vessel appears to have measured approximately 32 cm in width with wall thicknesses of 10 mm. Tempered with quartz sand, the specimen is unique among others recovered at Errol's Landing and Alexis Marcel's Island (Williams 1996, Table 13).

Site	Levels	Date	Laboratory
Kurupukari Falls (V111 – 2: 23)	45-60 cm	2080 +/- 70 B.P.	Beta 76246
	60-80 cm	2910 +/- 80 B.P.	Beta 76247
Makari Falls (V111 – 2: 32)	20-40 cm	90 +/- 50 B.P.	Beta 76249

(after Williams 1996)

Table 12. Radiocarbon Dates from Kurupukari and Makari Falls

Level	Sherds/level		Decorated sherds			Decorated rims	
	Plain	Decorated	Incised	Modeled	Painted	Flanged+Incised	Painted
0-15 cm			7	-	-	2	-
15-30 cm	777	25 3.2%	23	2	-	8	-
30-45 cm	329	61 18.5%	49	9	3	15	2
45-60 cm	106	6 5.6%	5	1	-	1	-
60-80 cm	9	-	-	-	-	-	-

(after Williams 1996)

Table 13. V111 – 2:23 Kurupukari Falls. Sherd Frequencies/Level

Siparuni River

Located on the right bank of the Siparuni River immediately below the waterfall is a habitation area excavated by Williams during his survey of the Iwokrama. A series of shovel probes and excavation of a 2 x 2 m test pit recovered a total of 552 sherds from the 15 cm levels. Level 0-15 cm contained a dense layer of humus under which lay silty yellowish soil. This level contained no cultural material. Level 15-30 cm was a more compacted silty yellowish soil with charcoal fragments and pottery sherds. Level 30-45 cm saw a gradual change in soil color from yellowish to pale orange with greater soil compaction and less cultural material. In addition to pottery, lithic flakes were noted throughout the deposit.

The ceramic inventory consisted of 552 sherds. Of these only 46 or 8.3% were decorated (Williams 1996). Tempering agents for both decorated and undecorated ceramics included quartz sand, crushed decomposed granite, and caraipé. Most sherd cores are dark tan in color with a range of hardness between 3.0 and 3.5 Moh scale. Decoration included a rare use of red and white slips, incision, stamping, fingernail impression, modeling, and unerased coils. There was no evidence of painted designs.

As to form, seven vessel shapes were recorded and include open bowls with direct rims and tapered, rounded, or beveled lips with mouth diameters of 12-40 cm and vessel wall thickness ranging between 4-8 mm; bowls or jars with incurvate walls and constricted mouths with direct rims and tapered, rounded, or beveled lips; mouth diameters of 16-24 cm and wall thicknesses of between 3.5 and 6 mm; bowls with constricted necks and wide, flaring rims with rounded, tapered or beveled lips having mouth diameters extending to 36 cm and vessel wall thicknesses between 5-6.5 mm; globular jars with constricted necks and wide everted rims with rounded or tapered lips and mouth diameters extending to a maximum of 60 cm while vessel walls range between 6-16 mm; globular jar or bottle with vertical or slightly incurvate collared neck having mouth diameter of 6 cm; bowl with constricted mouth and exteriorly thickened rim with mouth diameter of 12 cm and a vessel wall thickness of 5 mm; and a colander having perforations measuring 20-25 mm in diameter and set 12-25 mm apart (Williams n.d.). The decorated ceramics from Big "S" Falls include four types that in form resemble undecorated varieties: open bowls with direct or thickened rims which are painted red-on-white; deep bowls with vertical to incurvate walls with overlapping unerased coils 6-8 mm wide; a carinated bowl with incurvate collar and flanged rim decorated with a stamped lattice of lozenge-shaped motifs measuring up to 20 mm in diameter; and a jar lid having unerased coils and "U"-sectioned elements below rim exteriors. In general, the types represented are similar in form, style, and decoration to Taruma, Koriabo, and Rupununi phase materials (see Evans and Meggers 1960, Figs. 89,95; Plew n.d.; Plew and Peirera 2002; Williams 1996).

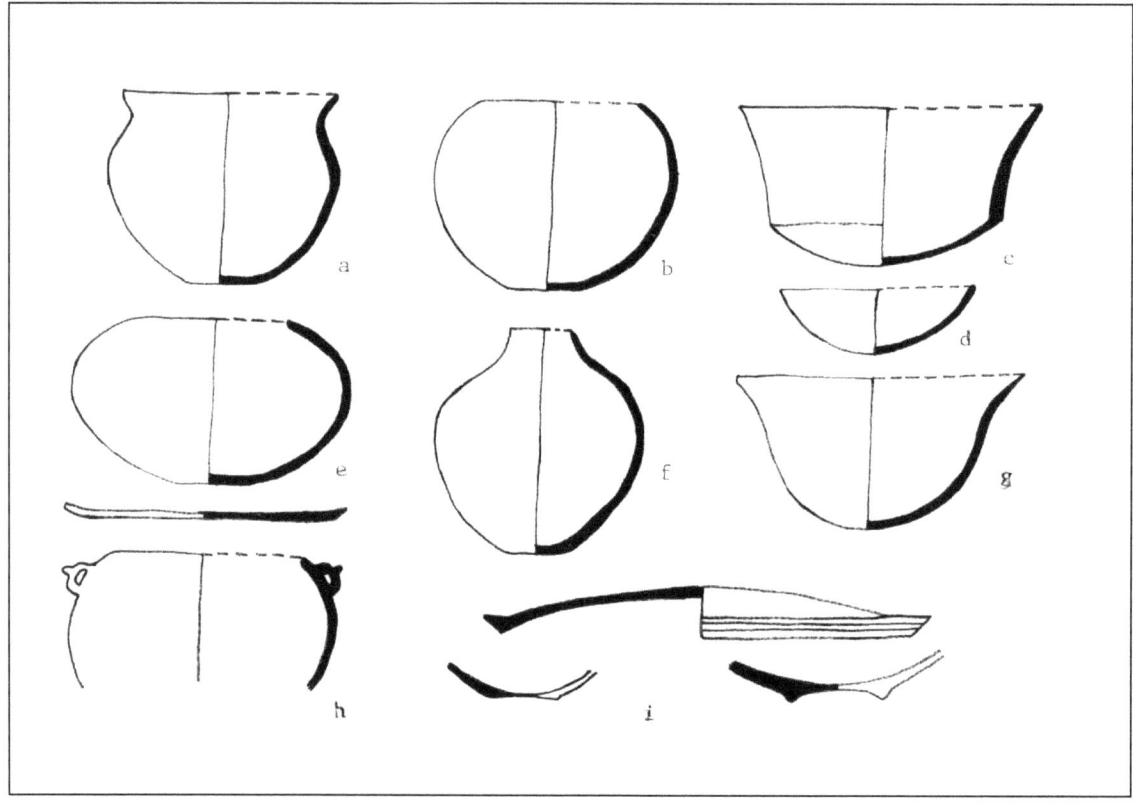

Figure 42. a-i, General Vessel forms from Kurupukari (after Williams 2004)

Figure 43. a-f, Kurupukari Incised and Modeled; g-h, Grooving; I, Fingernail Ridged; j, Scraped; k, brushed; l-m, Serial Finger Tip Impressions; n-q, Polychrome (after Williams 2004)

The Central Guyana Rainforest

Summary

Though the archaeology of Iwokrama remains in its infancy, a number of significant sites have been identified within the reserve (see Figure 39). Archaic and Horticultural occupations are documented by a total of twenty-nine sites that include habitations, manufacturing stations, groundstone basins, pollisoirs, and petroglyphs. While no evidence of Paleo-Indians has been identified, it appears likely that such evidence may come to light given the appearance of Paleo-Indians elsewhere in Guyana and the Amazonian basin. It seems likely that Paleo-Indians utilizing the northern Rupununi would have intruded into the Iwokrama forest as Paleo-Indian artifacts have been reported elsewhere in Guyana (see Williams 1985a, Plew 1997).

The Archaic Period, which dates between 7,000 and 3,500 years ago, suggests a pattern of broad spectrum foraging and a range of associated sites which are well documented within the reserve. Archaic period sites on the Essequibo include petroglyphs, sharpening grooves and a chipping station. Petroglyphs belonging to the Enumerative and Fish Trap Petroglyph Traditions (Williams 1985a) occur at Kurupukari Falls, Kurukupari Landing, Turtle Pond, Sharples Island, and Cuneiform Rock-1. On the Siparuni River, Archaic petroglyphs were recorded below the mouth of the Takatu River and at a number of other locations. In addition, a significant number of artificial stone depressions and sharpening grooves have been found at Pakutau Falls, Electric Eel Rock, Tapir Rock, and Trinity Rock.

On the Burro Burro River, Archaic petroglyphs, artificial depressions, and an Archaic chipping station have been found. Artificial depressions and sharpening grooves were most common at Black Rock, Unnamed Rock, Woodants Rock, and Dukali Falls. Most notably, Williams (1996) reports thousands of pieces of quartz debitage as well as choppers at Inscription Rock which may indicate that Iwokrama area was an important source of lithic raw materials. The Archaic settlement of Iwokrama indicates utilization of different resources in various locations within the forest and along the rivers. The range of site types suggests that Archaic peoples both processed local products and manufactured stone tools.

Some Archaic sites in Iwokrama and the North Rupununi are similar to some recently discovered sites at Petit Saut on the Middle Sinnamary River in French Guiana (Vacher, Jérémie, and Briand 1998). In particular, there are marked similarities to the types of pollisoirs and what appear to be manufacturing stations or workshop areas. The later have only recently been reported in the Rupununi area of Guyana (Plew and Pereira 2000). In general, the groundstone features resemble those described by Geijskes (1961:79-94) for the Coppename area in Suriname. This raises the question as to the age of such features in Guyana. Radiocarbon dates from the Sinnamary River area in French Guiana range between 1660 and 220 B.P., suggesting that they most probably occur in both the Archaic and later Horticultural periods. The implication for Iwokrama and the North Rupununi is that sites described by Williams (1985, 1996) as Archaic sites include the artifacts and feature inventories similar to those of the horticultural period.

The settlement pattern of the Archaic may be described as one in which sites were situated along major river courses and near falls and rock outcrops. Their location and size suggest that foraging populations utilized the fisheries and forest resources, the exploitation of which was made possible by stone tools produced from locally acquired materials. The recent discovery of aboriginal sites along tertiary drainages (Plew 2002) away from major rivers indicates an intensive use of Iwokrama.

The Horticultural Period, dating between 3,500 B.P. and the Historic period, is documented by eight habitation sites that include Errol's Landing, Alexis Marcel's Island, Reserve Base Camp (Field Station), Makari Falls, Martin's Island, David Andries Landing, and Kurukupari Falls (isolated find) on the Essequibo River and at Big "S" Falls on the Siparuni River. Excavations at sites on the Essequibo River, particularly those from Errol's Landing, documented a wide range of ceramic bowl and globular forms including carinated vessels. Though 90% of the ceramics from horticultural occupations in the reserve are undecorated (+90%), decorated wares include red-on-white painting, incision, punctation (noding), brushing, stamping, modeling, and fingernail impressions.

Test excavations at Big "S" Falls produced evidence of an assemblage of open and deep bowls and globular jars quite similar in form to those on the Essequibo River, particularly Errol's Landing at Kurukupari Falls. Though some vessels exhibited evidence of a possible but eroded red wash, the pottery from Big "S" Falls is undecorated. Most are similar to Koriabo, Taruma, and Rupununi types with undecorated (utilitarian) wares significantly more common. This may suggest an exchange relationship between these patterns.

Notably, test excavations at Errol's Landing (Beta 76246, as reported in Williams 1996) indicate a human presence in the reserve at about 3000 B.P. if not earlier. The recovery of early Polychrome Horizon Style ceramics may prove significant in understanding the origins and distribution of this ware in Guyana and the region. Recent discoveries near Toka Village indicate that similar wares were being produced locally or traded between the Iwokrama area and the north Rupununi. The settlement pattern in Iwokrama is one in which horticultural villages/encampments were located on larger river terraces and near falls and estuaries and suggests a continued emphasis upon fishing during the Horticultural period. In the Rupununi, some settlements were located on hilltops overlooking the savannah. Within the forest areas, caves and rockshelters appear to have commonly served as burial locations and for other ritual purposes.

THE ARCHAEOLOGY OF GUYANA

Drainage Sites		Paleo-Indian	Archaic	Horticultural	Historic
Essequibo		-	Kurupukari Landing	Errol's Landing	Haimara House
		-	Kurupukari Falls	Alexis Marcel's Island	Post Arinda
		-	Cuneiform Rock	Reserve Base Camp	-
		-	Turtle Pond	Makari Falls	-
		-	Sharples Island	Martin's Island	-
		-		Kurupukari Falls	-
Siparuni		-	Pakatau Falls	-	-
		-	Electric Eel Rock	-	-
		-	Tapir Rock	-	-
		-	Big "S" Falls	-	-
		-	Little "S" Falls	-	-
		-	Trinity Rock	-	-
Burro Burro		-	Black Rock	-	-
		-	Unnamed Rock	-	-
		-	Woodants Rocks	-	-
		-	Dukali Falls	-	-
		-	Inscription Rock	-	-

Table 14. General Chronology Of Iwokrama Sites

In general, archaeology in the reserve and in the adjacent North Rupununi area establishes an early Archaic antiquity and, as documented by excavations at Errol's Landing, early evidence of horticultural practice. This establishes a greater antiquity use of Iwokrama than in the surrounding area. Kurupukari Falls and other sites indicate a degree of permanency of occupation associated with fisheries and horticultural activities. The presence of the Enumerative and Fish Trap Petroglyph Traditions are noted in the reserve. Generally, depth and width of petroglyph gravures are notably deep and broad. Williams identifies the presence of the so-called Cuneiform glyph. As a sub-type (technique) of the Enumerative Tradition, this represents its first identification in Guyana.

The presence of the fish trap petroglyph is important since its distribution is known primarily from the rivers to the south. Its documentation in Iwokrama suggests that the pattern may be more widespread than earlier thought. Furthermore, its presence is indicative of the fisheries management strategy first described by Williams on the Kassikaityu River (1979b). Though Williams (1985a, 1996) has argued that the use of fisheries glyph markers is associated with periods of Holocene desiccation, it appears that some may be associated with seasonal water levels, which have undoubtedly varied over time.

Finally, the documentation of an extremely large number of artificial stone depressions and sharpening grooves and the presence of an Archaic Period quartz tool manufacturing station indicate a significant use of Iwokrama not only in exploitation of its fisheries and forest resources but also for extraction of tool stones such as the quartz deposits at Inscription Rock. This is most likely a strategy which extends into the Horticultural period.

On the basis of existing data, it appears that neither Iwokrama nor the North Rupununi saw a significant Paleo-Indian occupation. In contrast, considerable evidence indicates extensive use of the savannah and adjacent rain forest during the Archaic and later Horticultural periods. During these periods there is considerable similarity in the material culture and range of sites. An important issue is the degree of variability in local versus regional adaptations. The present level of archaeological investigations does not allow for observations regarding the influence of environmental change upon shifting procurement strategies of prehistoric peoples in the area.

At the present time, the absence of dated stratigraphic contexts prevents an adequate delineation of the more precise relationships between the settlement-subsistence strategies of Iwokrama and those of the North Rupununi. As such, future investigations should seek to more widely identify the distribution and range of site types within the areas and conduct excavations which permit the development of more detailed chronologies and allow for the description of a regional settlement regime. Such work should seek to identify archaeological features within sites and develop paleo-environmental data for purposes of assessing long-term variations in procurement strategies. More detailed archaeological research should provide important insights regarding the regional human ecology of the Iwokrama forest and adjacent savannah as well as of other areas throughout the Guianas.

XII. Guyana Prehistory In Review

The prehistory of Guyana has been divided into three major periods. The first, dating from at least 12,000 year ago, is the Paleo-Indian period associated with late Pleistocene peoples believed to have engaged in the hunting of large animals such as the giant ground sloth. During this time early peoples presumably migrated through southern Guyana into northeastern Brazil. Notably, no definite Paleo-Indian artifacts or sites document a pattern of big game hunting. More likely, late Paleo-Indians in the savannahs of southern Guyana were generalized foraging groups. Though little is known of these peoples, they produced well-crafted, triangular-bladed projectiles sometimes made from quartz and chert. As modern conditions developed some 7,000 years ago, Meso-Indian or Archaic hunter-gatherers appear on the northwest coast and in the Rupununi savannah.

Numerous shell middens on the coast and around the swamps of the northwest and Pomeroon areas reflect the extensive use of a variety of shellfish. Williams (1998) has defined what he describes as the Western Guiana Littoral, Early Archaic (7330-5960 B.P.), Middle Archaic (5960 B.P.--), and Late Archaic Periods (3550 B.P.--). These periods are correlated, as was the Paleo-Indian Period, with episodes of increasing and diminishing sea levels which alternately left significant portions of the coast inundated or exposed.

In northwest Guyana there is no evidence of Paleo-Indian occupation. The Archaic is characterized by the Alaka Phase dating between A.D. 1 and A.D. 500 and associated with an extensive exploitation of shellfish. The exploitation is well evidenced by several shell mounds found within the area that range up to 80 x 30 m and are between one and fifteen meters in height. The earliest known shell mound is the Pirika Mound radiocarbon-dated at ca. 7,300 B.P. Subsistence varied seasonally and over time but included use of snails, mussels, oysters, crabs, and conches as well as birds, fishes, and mammals. It is presumed that a range of plants, including palm, was utilized by local groups. The toolkit includes simple percussion-made choppers, hammerstones, and picks produced from andesite, quartz, and schist. Archaeological features of the early Archaic Alaka Phase as known from Barabina and other mound sites include fire-cracked rock, concentrations of lithic debris, hearths, storage pits, post molds, and burials. Evans and Meggers (1960: 63-64) note the appearance in the later part of the Alaka Phase of a few crudely made shell-tempered sherds of the type Wanaina Plain. This "incipient ceramic" period is associated with groundstone tools that include celts, mortars, manos, pestles and grinding stones. Mound burials of adults and children document preferential treatment of the dead and suggest some degree of social differentiation.

The Archaic shell mounds of the Northwest are important in establishing the appearance of pottery and horticulture in Guyana. The appearance of large village sites and well-made pottery marks the beginning of the Mabaruma Phase dating between A.D. 500 and A.D. 1600 (Evans and Meggers 1960:122). In some instances, sites range to more than 17,000 square meters. In addition to pottery, assemblages are characterized by manos, metates, polished celts, and possible hoes. Mabaruma pottery, replaced by sand-tempered Hosororo pottery in the later part of the phase, marks the beginning of the Formative period.

Williams (1998) recently argued for an earlier beginning of the Mabaruma Phase at about 1600 B.CA. on the basis of pottery recovered at Barabina and at Hosororo Mounds. Further work will determine if Williams' claims regarding an earlier beginning of the Mabaruma Phase are supported. This work will also provide resolution to the Williams-Roosevelt debate (1997). The Koriabo Phase materials dating from around A.D. 1200 overlaps with the Mabaruma Phase. Associated with sites ranging to 7,400 square meters, the phase is characterized by three plain pottery types distinguished by temper and two decorated types which include incised and scraped decoration with low appliqué, nubbins, and anthropomorphic faces. A material culture that includes ceramic pot rests, griddle fragments, celts, and chisels completes a toolkit reflecting horticultural activities.

The archaeology of the Northeastern portion of Guyana, while not well-known, is characterized by the Abary Phase defined by Evans and Meggers (1960) and by Hertenrits culture defined by Boomert (1977) in Suriname. The Abary Phase, consisting of sites between the Abary and Berbice Rivers, is a forest adaptation utilizing interior and perhaps coastal resources. The settlement pattern includes seasonal use of primary and secondary waterways allowing for the utilization of seasonally varied landscapes and resources. The pottery types Tiger Island, Taurakuli, and Abary Plain occur with successive predominance within the area and are distinguished by cariapé, sherd, and sand temper. Steatite-tempered Hotokwai Plain establishes the contemporaneity of the Abary Phase with the Mabaruma of the Northwest. In the east is a second pattern defined by Boomert as Hertenrits culture. While settlement, subsistence, and material culture are similar to those of the Abary Phase, the presence of habitation mounds and raised fields is notable. The Joanna Mound on the Canje River in Guyana measures 90 m in diameter and rises some 2.5 m above ground level and is encircled by a moat-like feature. The presence of daub at a number of mounds suggests mud walls. The existence of nearly 800 raised field mounds in the vicinity of Fort Nassau on the Berbice River suggests significant horticultural activity within the area.

To the south, the archaeology of the Rupununi Savannahs suggests a possible early Paleo-Indian presence and Archaic and Horticultural occupations. The Paleo-Indian presence is evidenced by paleo-type points found near the Ireng River and from the vicinity of Mariwau in the south savannahs. Though evidence is extremely limited, the nature of the Pleistocene environment suggests the likelihood that the area was inhabited by early peoples. In contrast with Williams' (1985) assertions that early Paleo-Indians were big game hunters, it seems likely that the Rupununi is associated with a strategy of Paleo-Indian foraging. The Archaic pattern may date as early as 5,000 B.CA. and is characterized by a range of chipped and portable and permanent groundstone artifacts and features/permanent artifacts that include grinding surface/depressions and sharpening grooves (*pollisoirs*). Geometric rock alignments, stone piles (cairns), and circles are common. At Aishalton and Makatau Mountain, 30 petroglyph sites include bimorphic and geometric motifs. Elements there were inscribed using a broad line and deep groove technique that often combined dots and furrows, placing them in settings with bimorphic and geometric motifs. Williams (1979a, 1985a) argues that varied combinations of motifs imply a sequential reading of elements which signed the presence of resources in different areas and may have linked rituals related to subsistence. His excavations along the margins of the granite boulders report manufactured stone tools he believes were employed in producing rock art (Plew n.d.).

The Horticultural Period is associated with the appearance of pottery of the Rupununi Phase identified with the historic Makushi and Wapishana, by the occurrence of 18th and 19th century European trade goods. Two pottery types, Rupununi Plain and Kanuku Plain, constitute the majority of the ceramic inventory. Forms include deep bowls with steep walls, globular bowls and jars with rounded walls and incurving and rounded lips, and carinated vessels forming round to sloping shoulders. Surface color ranges typically from orange to reddish orange to reddish brown. The two types are distinguished by Rupununi Plain, which has a gray core. Rare sherds have decoration in the form of appliqué, punctuates, white paint, and white and red slips. Ceramic artifacts include pottery rests, disks, and anthropomorphic figurines. Chipped and groundstone artifacts include anvils, choppers, grooved axes, hoes, manos, metates, hammerstones, and stone bowl fragments.

The settlement pattern includes habitation sites (open villages), manufacturing stations, fishing sites, ceremonial sites (rock alignments), cemetery sites, and rock art locations. Recent investigations suggest a broader range of activities and site types within the area as evidenced by the elaborate cemeteries at Shiriri Mountain and hilltop villages near Toka. The diversity of Rupununi settlement reflects the varied nature of the savannah environment in which Amerindians utilized open terrain along streams and rivers for habitation, adjacent bush islands for farming or gardening, and higher elevations within the mountains for ritual practice and for cemeteries.

In the central Guyana Iwokrama rainforest, Archaic and Horticultural occupations include habitation sites, manufacturing stations, groundstone basins and pollisoirs, and petroglyphs. Though no evidence of Paleo-Indians has been identified, their presence in surrounding areas is known. It seems likely that Paleo-Indians utilizing the northern Rupununi would have intruded into the Iwokrama forest.

The Archaic Period, which dates between 7,000 and 3,500 years ago, suggests a pattern of broad spectrum foraging. On the Essequibo, Archaic period sites include petroglyphs, sharpening grooves, and a chipping station. Petroglyphs belong to the Enumerative and Fish Trap Petroglyph Tradition (Williams 1985a) and occur at many locations including Kurupukari Falls and Cuneiform Rock-1. On the Siparuni River, Archaic petroglyphs and large numbers of artificial stone depressions and sharpening grooves have been documented at Pakatau Falls, Electric Eel Rock, and Tapir Rock. On the Burro Burro River, many thousands of pieces of quartz debitage as well as choppers at Inscription Rock have been found. The Archaic settlement of Iwokrama indicates use of a variety of locations within the forest and along the rivers and a range of site types suggesting that Archaic peoples were both processing local products and manufacturing stone tools.

The settlement pattern of the Archaic is one in which sites were situated along major river courses and near falls and rock outcrops. Local foraging populations exploited the fisheries and other forest resources using stone tools produced from locally acquired materials. The recent discovery of aboriginal sites along tertiary drainages (Plew 2002) away from major rivers may indicate use of large areas within the forest.

The Horticultural Period dates between 3,500 B.P. and the Historic period. Excavations at sites on the Essequibo River, particularly those from Errol's Landing, document a wide range of ceramic bowl and globular forms including carinated vessels. Though ninety percent of the ceramics are undecorated, rare decoration includes the use of red-on-white painting, incisions, punctation (noding), brushing, stamping, modeling, and fingernail incisions. Test excavations at Big "S" Falls produced evidence of an assemblage of open and deep bowls and globular jars quite similar in form to those on the Essequibo River, particularly Errol's Landing at Kurukupari Falls. Most are similar to Koriabo, Taruma and Rupununi types with undecorated (utilitarian) wares significantly more common.

Test excavations at Errol's Landing (Beta 76246, as reported in Williams 1996) indicate a human presence in the reserve at about 3000 B.P., if not earlier. The recovery of early Polychrome Horizon Style ceramics may prove significant in understanding the origins and distribution of this ware in Guyana and in the region. Recent discoveries near Toka Village indicate that similar wares were being produced locally or traded between the Iwokrama area and the north Rupununi. The settlement pattern in Iwokrama includes horticultural villages/encampments located on larger river terraces and near falls and estuaries, suggesting a continued emphasis upon fishing during the horticultural period.

In summary, the archaeology of Guyana documents considerable variation in human occupations that, spanning several thousand years, is characterized by a variety of settlement-subsistence patterns that include the rainforest, shellfisheries, and the mixed resources of the savannahs. The material culture lifeways of the numerous archaeological phases are equally diverse and demonstrate considerable local innovation. At the present time, the existence of only a few dated stratigraphic contexts prevents detailed delineation of the temporal distribution, lifeways, and material cultures of prehistoric Amerindians across Guyana. Future investigations must seek to more precisely identify the distribution and range of site types within major physiographic and environmental areas and conduct excavations to permit the development of more detailed chronologies. Such work must identify archaeological features within sites and develop paleo-environmental data for purposes of assessing long-term variations in procurement strategies. More detailed archaeological research will provide important insights into the regional human ecology of Guyana and as such contribute significantly to the archaeology of the Guianas and of adjacent areas.

References Cited

Absy, M.L. 1985. Palynology of Amazonia: The History of the Forest as Revealed by the Palynological Record. In *Amazonia* edited by G.T. Prance and T.E. Lovejoy, Pergamon Press.

Amerindian Research Unit 1992. The Material Culture of the Wapishana of the South Rupununi Savannahs in 1989. University of Guyana, Georgetown.

Amerindian Research Unit 2003. A Look at the Archaeology of Guyana: Fifty Years After Osgood. University of Guyana, Georgetown.

Baldwin, R. 1946. Report of the District Commissioner, Rupununi, for the Quarter Ending 31st March 1946.

Boomert, A. 1975. Archeologishe Vindplaatzen in Suriname. Rapport Surnaams Museum, Archaeologishe Dienst 1. Paramaribo.

Boomert, A. 1977. Prehistorie. In Encyclopedie van Suriname, CA.F.A. Bruijning, J. Voorhoeve and W. Gordijin, editors, pp. 505-515, Amsterdam/Brussels.

Boomert, A. 1981. The Taruma Phase of Southern Suriname. *Archaeology and Anthropology* 4(1 and 2): 104-157.

Brett, W. H. 1868. *The Indian Tribes of Guyana: Their Condition and Habits.* Bell and Dalby, New York.

Brown, C.A.B. 1873. Indian Picture Writing in British Guiana. *Journal of the Royal Anthropological Institute* 2:254-261.

Brown, C.A.B. 1876. *Canoe and Camp Life in British Guiana.* Edward Stanford, London.

Brown, K.S. 1977. Centro de Evolucâó, Refugios Quaternarious, e Conservâcaó de Patrimonios Genéticos no Região Neotropical: Padrões de Diferenciacó em Ithomiinae. *Acta Amazônica* 7(1): 75-137.

Brown, K.S., and A.N. Ab'Saber 1979. Ice-Age Refuges and Evolution in the Neotropics: Correlation of Paleoclimatological, Geomorphological and Pedological Data with Modern Biological Endemism. *Paleoclimas* 5.

Bryan, A. L. 1991. The Fluted-Point Tradition in the Americas—One of Several Adaptations to Late Pleistocene American Environments. In *Clovis: Origins and Adaptations*, edited by R. Bonnichsen and K.L. Turnmire, editors, Center for the Study of Early Americans, Corvallis.

Butt, Audrey J. 1954. Systems of Belief in Relation to Social Structure and Organization with Reference to the Carib Speaking Tribes of the Guianas. Ph.D. Dissertation, Oxford University, London.

Dubelaar, CA. N., and J .P. Berrange 1979. Some Recent Petroglyph Finds in Southern Guyana. *Archaeology and Anthropology* 2 (1): 60-76.

Evans, CA. and B. J. Meggers 1960. Archeological Investigations in British Guiana. Bureau of American Ethnology. Bulletin 197. Smithsonian Institution, Washington D.C.

Evans, CA., B. J. Meggers, and J. M. Cruxent 1957. Preliminary Results of Archeological Investigations Along the Orinoco and Ventuari Rivers, Venezuela. Actas del XXXIII Congreso Internacional de Americanists, San José, 1958: 359-369.

Farabee, W. CA. 1918. *The Central Arawaks.* Anthropological Publications of the University of Pennsylvania Museum, Philadelphia.

Farabee, W. CA. 1924. *The Central Caribs.* Anthropological Publications of the University of Pennsylvania Museum, Philadelphia.

Fock, N. 1963. Wai-Wai: Religion and Society of an Amazonian Tribe. *Ethnographic Series, 8.* Copenhagen: The National Museum of Denmark.

Forte, J. 1990. The Case of the Barama Caribs of Guyana Restudied. *Social and Economic Studies* 39(1): 203-217. Kingston: University of the West Indies.

Forte, J. 1996a. *About Guyanese Indians.* University of Guyana, Georgetown.

Forte, J. 1996b. *Thinking About Amerindians.* University of Guyana, Georgetown.

Forte, J., and I. Melville 1989. *Amerindian Testimonies.* Boise State University, Boise.

Frikel, P. 1961. Fases culturais e aculturaçao intertribal no Tumucumaque, *Boletin do Museu Paranese Emílio Goeldi Anthropologia* 16, Belem.

Frikel, P. 1969. Tradition und Archäologie im Tumuk-Humak/Nordbrasilien. *Zeitschrift für Ethnologie* 94: 103-130.

Geijskes, D.CA. 1961. Archaeologishe Vondsten van de Coppename in Suriname. *Mededeling Suriname Museum* Nr. 4: 79-94.

Gillin, John 1936. The Barama River Caribs of British Guiana. *Peabody Museum Papers in Archaeology and Ethnology* 14(2): 1-274.

Goodland, E.A. 1964. The Mound. *Journal of the British Guiana Museum and Zoo* 39:9-17.

Goodland, E. A. 1976. Report on Inscribed Rock at Aishalton, South Rupununi Savannah, Guyana. The Goodland Papers. Manuscript, University of Guyana Library, Georgetown.

Haffer, J. 1969. Speciation in Amazonian Forest Birds. *Science* 165: 131-137.

Haffer, J. 1982. General Aspects of Refuge Theory. In *Biological Diversification in the Tropics,* edited by G.T. Prance, Columbia University Press, New York, pp. 6-24.

Hanif, M. 1967. Petroglyphs in the Rupununi. *Timehri* 43: 19-27.

Harris, CA. A. and J.J. de Villiers. 1911. *Storm van's Gravesande: The Rise of British Guiana.* 2 vols. Leichtenstein: Klans Reprint, Liechtenstein.

Henderson, G. 1952. Stone Circles and Tiger's Liars. *Timehri* 31:62-66.

Hilbert P. 1982. Pottery from the Cumina River and Its Affiliations with Koriabo Phase of Guyana. *Journal of Archaeology and Anthropology* 5(2): 74-81.

Hurault, J .M., P. Frenay and Y. Raoux. 1956. Pétroglyphs et assemblages de pierres dans le Sud-Est de la Guyanne Française. *Journal de la Société des Américanistas* 52:157-166.

Hurt, W. R. 1960. The Cultural Complexes from the Logoa Santa Region, Brazil. *American Anthropologist* 52(4):560-585.

Hurt, W. R. 1977. The Edge Trimmed Tool Tradition of Northwest South America. In *For the Director: Research Essays in Honor of James B. Griffen*, edited by Charles E. Cleland, pp. 268-294, University of Michigan, Ann Arbor.

Im Thurn, E.F. 1883. *Among the Indians of Guiana*. Kegan, Paul, Trench and Company, London.

Im Thurn, E. F. 1884. Notes on West Indian Stone Implements, and other Indian Relics. *Timehri*, 103-137.

Jansma, M.J. 1981. Diatom Analysis of a Section in the Barabina Shell Midden. *Archaeology and Anthropology* 4(1-2): 37-38.

Lynch, T. F. 1998. The Paleoindian and Archaic Stages in South America: Zones of Continuity and Zones of Segregation. In *Explorations in American Archaeology: Essays in Honor of Wesley R. Hurt*, edited by Mark G. Plew, University Press of America, Lanham, Maryland.

Meggers, B. J. 1971. *Amazonia: Man and Culture in a Counterfeit Paradise*. Aldine, Chicago.

Meggers, B.J. 1994. Biogeographical Approaches to Reconstructing the Prehistory of Amazonia. *Biogeographica* 70(3): 97-110.

Meggers, B. J. and CA. Evans. 1957. Archeological Investigations at the Mouth of the Amazon. Smithsonian Institution, Bureau of American Ethnology, Bulletin 167. Washington, D.CA.

Meggers B.J., and E. Miller 2003. Hunter and Gatherers in Amazonia During the Pleistocene Transition. In *Under the Canopy: The Archaeology of the Tropical Rain Forests*. Edited by Julio Mercader, pp. 291-316. Rutgers University Press, New Brunswick.

Menezes, Mary Noel 1979. *The Amerindians in Guyana 1803-1873: A Documentary History*. Frank Cass, London.

Mentor, G. 1984. Shepariymo: The Political Economy of a Wai-Wai Village. Ph.D. Dissertation, University of Sussex.

Mentor, G. 1988. The Relevance of Myth. The Department of Culture, Georgetown.

Mentor, G. 1995. Peccary Meat and Power Among the Wai-Wai Indians of Guyana. *Journal of Archaeology and Anthropology* 10: 19-35.

Meyers, I. 1944. The Makushi of British Guiana: A Study in Culture Contact. Part I. *Timehri* 26: 66-77.

Meyers, I. 1946. The Makushi of British Guiana: A Study in Culture Contact. Part II. *Timehri* 27: 16-38.

Moran, E. 1993. *Through Amazonian Eyes: The Human Ecology of Amazonian Populations*. University of Iowa Press, Iowa City.

Osgood, CA. 1946. British Guiana Archaeology to 1945. *Yale University Publications in Anthropology* No. 36, New Haven, Connecticut.

Parsons J. and W. Deneven 1967. Pre-Columbian Ridged Fields. In *New World Archaeology*, pp. 240-248.

Plew, M. G. 1997. Recent Evidence of Paleoindian Occupations in the Lower Amazon: Implications for the Early Prehistory of Guyana. Paper Presented at the 24th Annual Conference of the Idaho Archaeological Society, Albertson's College, Caldwell.

Plew, M. G. 2002a. A Report on Archaeological Survey in the Iwokrama Mountains with Recommendations Regarding the Development of Protocols Relating To Archaeological Sites, Report on File, Iwokrama International Centre for Rainforest Conservation and Development, 10 pp.

Plew, M. G. 2002b. Field Notes, Kurukupari Falls and Field Station Investigations, October 2002.

Plew, M.G. 2003. Archaeology in the Iwokrama Rainforest, Guyana. *Antiquity*, Vol. 77, No. 298.

Plew, M.G. n.d. The Archaeology of Iwokrama and The North Rupununi. In *Iwokrama* Edited by Leo Joseph, Volume 154, pp. 7-28. Proceedings of the Natural Academy of Sciences of Philadelphia.

Plew, M.G., and J. Forte 1998. *A Bibliography of Guyana Anthropology*. Boise State University, Boise.

Plew, M. G., K. Mercer and T. Sundell. 2001. A Report on the Archaeological Survey of Areas Near Moco-Moco Creek and Imprenza, Rupununi Savannahs, Guyana. Report on File, Walter Roth Museum Anthropology, Georgetown, 26 pp.

Plew, M. G., and G. Pereira. 2000. Archaeological Survey of the Shiriri Mountain Area, South Rupununi Savannahs, Guyana. *Journal of Anthropology and Archaeology* 13: 1-7.

Plew, M. G. and G. Pereira. 2002. A Report on Archaeological Survey in the Vicinity of Toka and Yupukari Villages North Rupununi. Report on File, Walter Roth Museum of Anthropology, Georgetown, 29 pp.

Plew, M. G. and S. Saras. 2001. Archaeological Survey in the Vicinity of Shulinab Village and Inaja, Southern Guyana. Report on File, Walter Roth Museum of Anthropology, Georgetown, 19 pp.

Prance, G.T. 1973. Phytogeographic Support for the Theory of Pleistocene Forest Refuges in the Amazon Basin, Based on Evidence from Distribution Patterns in *Caryocaraceae, Chrysobalanaceae, Dichapetelaceae* and *Lecythidaceae. Acta Amazonicas.* 3(3): 103-137.

Prance, G.T. 1982. Forest Refuges: Evidence from Woody Angiosperms. In *Biological Diversification in the Tropics*, edited by G.T. Prance. Columbia University Press, New York, pp. 137-158.

Poonai, N. O. 1962. Archaeological Sites on the Corentyne Coast. *Journal of the British Guiana Museum and Zoo.* 33: 52-53.

REFERENCES CITED

Poonai, N. O. 1970. *Stone Age Guyana: A Survey of Archeological Investigations in Guyana and Adjacent Lands*. National History and Arts Council, Georgetown.

Rivière, P. G. 1984. Individual and Society in Guiana. A Comparative Study of Amerindian Social Organization. *Cambridge Studies in Social Anthropology*, 51. Cambridge University Press, Cambridge.

Roosevelt, A. CA. 1980. *Parmana: Maize and Manioc Subsistence Along the Amazon and Orinoco*. Academic Press, New York.

Roosevelt, A. CA. 1995. Early Pottery in the Amazon: Twenty Years of Scholarly Obscurity. In *The Emergence of Pottery: Technology and Innovation in Ancient Societies*, edited by W. Barnett and J. Hoopes, pp. 115-132. Smithsonian Institution Press, Washington, D.C.

Roosevelt, A. CA. 1997a. The Demise of the Alaka Initial Ceramic Phase Has Been Greatly Exaggerated: Response to D. Williams. *American Antiquity* 62(2):353-364.

Roosevelt, A. CA., 1997b. Paleoindian and Archaic Occupations in the Lower Amazon, Brazil: A Summary and Comparison. In *Explorations of American Archaeology: Essays in Honor of Wesley R. Hurt*, edited by Mark G. Plew, University Press of America, Lanham, Maryland.

Roosevelt, A. CA., R. A. Housley, M. Imazio da Silveira, S. Maranca and R. Johnson 1991. Eight Millennium Pottery from a Prehistoric Shell Midden in the Brazilian Amazon. *Science* 254:1621-1624.

Roosevelt, A. CA., M. Lima da Costa, CA. Lopes Machado, M. Michab, N. Mercier, H. Vallada, J. Silva, B. Chernoff, D.S. Reese, J.A. Holman, N. Toth and K. Schick. 1996. Paleoindian Cave Dwellers in the Americas: The Peopling of the Americas. *Science* 272:373-384.

Roth, V. 1944. A Stone Age Bead Factory on the Mahaica River. *Timehri* 26: 42-48.

Roth, W.E. 1915. An Inquiry into the Animism and Folklore of the Guiana Indians. 30th *Annual Report of the Bureau of American Ethnology*, Washington, D.C., pp. 103-386.

Roth, W. E. 1924. An Introductory Study of the Arts, Crafts and Customs of the Guiana Indians. 38th *Annual Report of the Bureau of American Ethnology*, Washington, D.C.

Roth, W. 1929. Additional Studies of the Arts, Crafts, and Costumes of the Guiana Indians. Smithsonian Institution, *Bureau of American Ethnology*, Bulletin 91. Washington, D.C.

Rouse, I. and L. Allaire 1978. Caribbean. In *Chronologies in New World Archaeology*, edited by R.E. Taylor and CA.W. Meighan, Academic Press, New York, pp. 431-481.

Schomburgk, W. H. 1841. Report on the Third Expedition into the Interior of Guyana, Comprising the Journey to the Sources of the Essequibo. *Journal of the Royal Geographical Society*, 15: 1-104, London.

Siegel, P.E. 1990. Demographic and Architectural Retrodiction: An Ethnoarchaeological Case Study in South American Tropical Lowlands. *Latin American Antiquity* 1:319-346.

Simoes, M. 1976. Nota sobre duas Pontas de Projetil da Bacia Tapajos (Para). *Boletim do Museu Paraense Emílio Geoldi*, N.S. 62, Belém.

Simon, G. n.d. Field Notes and Map Regarding Raised Field Features near Fort Nassua. On File, Walter Roth Museum of Anthropology.

Sinoli, H.1984.The Amazon and Its Main Affluents: Hydrography, Morphology of River Courses and River Types. In *The Amazon: Limnology and Landscape Ecology of a Mighty Tropical River and Its Basin.* Edited by H. Sinoli, pp. 127-165. Dordrecht: W. Junk.

Stahl, P. W. (ed.) 1994. *Archaeology in the Lowland American Tropics*. Cambridge University Press, Cambridge.

Steward, J. H. 1949. South American Cultures: An Interpretive Summary. In *Handbook of South American Indians*, vol. 5, edited by J.H. Steward, pp. 669-772. Bureau of American Ethnology, Washington, D.C.

Toro, E. 1905. *Por las selvas de Guayana*, Caracas.

Thompson, A. 1979. Discovery of a New Mound with Remains of Aboriginal Inhabitants of the Abary Area. *Journal of Archaeology and Anthropology* 2(2): 149-150.

Van Andel, T.J. 1967. The Orinoco Delta. *Journal of Sedimentary Petrology* 37(2): 297-310.

Van der Hammen, T. 1963. A Palynological Study of the Quaternary of British Guiana. *Leidse Geologische Mededelingen* 29: 125-180.

Van der Hammen, T, and M.L. Absy 1994. Amazonia During the Last Glacial. *Paleogeography, Paleoclimatology and Paleoecology* 109: 247-261.

Vacher, S., S. Jérémie and J. Briand. 1998. *Amérindians du Sinnamary (Guyane): Archéologie en forêt équatoriale*. Editions de La Maison des Sciences de L'Homme. Paris.

Verrill, A. H. 1918. Prehistoric Mounds and Relics of the North West District of British Guiana. *Timehri* 5, pp. 11-20, Georgetown.

Verstaag, A. H. 1983.Raised Field Complexes and Associated Settlements in the Coastal Plain of Western Suriname. In *Drained Field Agricultre in Central and South America.* Edited by J.P. Darch, BAR International Series 189: 237-251.

Whitehead, N.L. 1996. Amazonian Archaeology: Searching for Paradise? A Review of the Recent Literature and Fieldwork. *Journal of Archaeological Research* 4(3): 241-264.

Williams, D. n.d.a. Archaeological Reconnaissance on the Middle Mazaruni River. Unpublished Manuscript on File, Walter Roth Museum of Anthropology, Georgetown.

Williams, D. n.d.b. Archaeological Reconnaissance on the Potaro River. Unpublished Manuscript on File, Walter Roth Museum of Anthropology, Georgetown.

Williams, D. n.d.c. Archaeological Reconnaissance on the Essequibo River. Unpublished Manuscript on File, Walter Roth Museum of Anthropology, Georgetown.

Williams, D. 1978a. A Stemmed Projectile Point from the Semang River. *Journal of Anthropology and Archaeology* 1 (1): 55.

Williams, D. 1978b. Test Pits at Itabru, Berbice River. *Journal of Archaeology and Anthropology* 1(1): 34-35.

Williams, D. 1979a. A Report on Preceramic Lithic Artifacts in the South Rupununi Savannahs. *Journal of Anthropology and Archaeology* 2 (1): 10-53.

Williams, D. 1979b. Pre-ceramic Fish Traps on the Upper Essequibo: Report on the Survey of Unusual Petroglyphs on the Upper Essequibo and Kassikaityu Rivers 12-28 March 1979. *Journal of Anthropology and Archaeology* 2(2) 125-140.

Williams, D. 1979c. Controlled Resource Exploitation in Contrasting Neo-tropical Environments Evidenced by Meso-Indian Petroglyphs in Southern Guyana. *Journal of Archaeology and Anthropology* 2: 141-148.

Williams, D. 1981a. Excavation of the Barambina Shell Mound North West District: An Interim Report. *Archaeology and Anthropology* 2(2):125-140.

Williams, D. 1982. Some Subsistence Implications of Holocene Climate Change in Northwestern Guyana. *Archaeology and Anthropology* 5(2):83-93.

Williams, D. 1985a. Petroglyphs in the Prehistory of North Amazonia and the Antilles. *Advances in World Archaeology* 4:335-387.

Williams, D. 1985b. *Ancient Guyana*. Ministry of Culture, Georgetown.

Williams, D. 1992. Arcaico en el noroeste de Guyana y los comienzos de la horticultura. In *Prehistoric Sudamericana. Nuevas Perspectivas*, edited by B. J. Meggers, Taraxacum, Washington, D.C.

Williams, D. 1995. *Pages in Guyanese Prehistory*. Walter Roth Museum of Anthropology, Georgetown.

Williams, D. 1996. Iwokrama: Archaeological Studies. The Commonwealth and Government of Guyana Rain Forest Programme. Unpublished Manuscript on File, Walter Roth Museum of Anthropology, Georgetown.

Williams, D. 1997a. The Mabaruma Phase: Origin Characterization and Chronology. *Archaeology and Anthropology* 11.

Williams, D. 1997b. Early Pottery in the Amazon: A Correction. *American Antiquity* 62(2):342-352.

Williams, D. 1998. The Archaic Colonization of the Western Guiana Littoral and Its Aftermath. *Journal of Archeology and Anthropology* 12(1): 22-41.

Williams, D. 2004. *Prehistoric Guiana*. Ian Randle Publishers, Kingston.

Wishart, J 1982a. A Note on Abary Phase House Construction. *Journal of Archaeology and Anthropology* 5(1): 68-69.

Wishart J. 1982b. Recht-door-Zee: A Site of the Abary Phase on the West Bank Demerara. *Journal of Archaeology and Anthropology* 5(2): 119-124.

Yde, J. 1965. Material Culture of the Waiwai. *Ethnographic Series*, 10. National Museum of Denmark, Copenhagen.

www.ingramcontent.com/pod-product-compliance
Ingram Content Group UK Ltd.
Pitfield, Milton Keynes, MK11 3LW, UK
UKHW061213180426
11947UKWH00029B/2021